# FORMING
# ALLIANCES

## Working Together to Achieve Mutual Goals

by Linda Hoskins and Emil Angelica

FIELDSTONE
ALLIANCE

SAINT PAUL,
MINNESOTA

We would like to thank
The David and Lucile Packard Foundation
for support of this publication.

D1360122

Fieldstone Alliance is committed to strengthening the
performance of the nonprofit sector. Through the syn-
ergy of its consulting, training, publishing, and research
and demonstration projects, Fieldstone Alliance provides solutions to issues facing nonprofits, funders, and
the communities they serve. Fieldstone Alliance was
formerly Wilder Publishing and Wilder Consulting departments of the Amherst H. Wilder Foundation. If you
would like more information about Fieldstone Alliance
and our services, please contact Fieldstone Alliance, 60
Plato Boulevard East, Suite 150, Saint Paul, MN 55107,
651-556-4500

We hope you find this book useful! For information about
other Fieldstone Alliance publications, please see the order form on the last page or contact:

Fieldstone Alliance
60 Plato Boulevard East
Suite 150
Saint Paul, MN 55107
800-274-6024
www.FieldstoneAlliance.org

Edited by Vincent Hyman
Text designed by Kirsten Nielsen
Cover designed by Rebecca Andrews

Manufactured in the United States of America
First printing, August 2005

**Library of Congress Cataloging-in-Publication Data**

Hoskins, Linda, 1951–
  Forming alliances : working together to achieve mutual goals /
by Linda Hoskins and Emil Angelica.
     p. cm.
  Includes bibliographical references.
  ISBN-13: 978-0-940069-46-6 (pbk.)
  ISBN-10: 0-940069-46-6 (pbk.)
  1. Nonprofit organizations--Management. 2. Strategic alliances
(Business)--Management. 3. Business networks--Management.
I. Angelica, Emil, 1946– II. Title.

  HD62.6.H67 2005
  658'.048--dc22

                    2005012678

Printed on recycled paper
30% post-consumer waste

## About the Authors

LINDA HOSKINS, a partner in Community Consulting Group in Minneapolis, Minnesota, was a senior consultant with Wilder Center for Communities for five years. Linda works with local nonprofit organizations, government agencies, and businesses on event design and management, community engagement, strategic planning, board development, and organization assessment. She is a coauthor of *The Wilder Nonprofit Field Guide to Community Forums: Engaging Citizens, Mobilizing Communities*. Linda has degrees in microbiology and nonprofit management and is a certified mediator through CDR & Associates.

EMIL ANGELICA is a partner with the Community Consulting Group in Minneapolis, Minnesota, and was a principal consultant with Wilder Center for Communities for more than eighteen years. He has more than twenty years' experience in providing consulting and training services in the topics of board and staff development, strategic planning, program evaluation, policy and community development, and nonprofit management. He has worked on a broad range of mergers, collaborations, and projects for refugee and immigrant communities. He is known as a national speaker and trainer, and is the author of *The Wilder Nonprofit Field Guide to Crafting Effective Mission and Vision Statements* and coauthor of *Coping with Cutbacks: The Nonprofit Guide to Success When Times Are Tight*. He recently completed a commission as a Fulbright Scholar in Cyprus. Emil has degrees in finance, management, and philosophy.

# Acknowledgements

This book is dedicated, with respect and gratitude, to our many partners, clients, and colleagues who have worked together to improve their communities and shared what they learned along the way with us.

Many people helped to make this book a reality.

We would like to thank Vince Hyman, Fieldstone Alliance, for his excellent support, advice, and editing skills throughout the year-long process of writing this book.

We also thank the following people who reviewed this book and gave us invaluable feedback on their experiences with alliances—David La Piana, La Piana Associates; Debbie Jackson; Karen Ray, Karen Ray Associates; and Tom Borrup, Community and Cultural Development.

And we want to offer thanks to our colleagues, Monica Herrera, Barb Rose, and many others who have provided us with moral, intellectual, and practical support in the writing of this book. A special note of appreciation and recognition goes to our gifted colleagues Carol Lukas, Fieldstone Alliance, and Chris Kloth, ChangeWorks of the Heartland, for providing us with frameworks that helped us represent some of the ideas in this book.

Linda is especially grateful to Jim, Brian, Chris, and friend Connie Knight who have encouraged her to live life to its fullest.

Emil thanks Ethan and Carmen for their continued patience listening to his consulting stories, some of which are reflected in this book, and Marion's tolerance for serving as a sounding board when partnership consulting projects don't go as planned.

# Contents

# Introduction

When faced with the daily challenges of managing a nonprofit organization, leaders may find it counterintuitive to look for partners as a first strategy for accomplishing their own mission most efficiently. That's too bad, because alliances often lead to solving the organization's needs and to addressing the needs of the community in ways that bring forth more resources and creative options than could be imagined. This book addresses three important questions posed by leaders who want to work in partnership with others to solve community issues:

- How do I engage others in forming an alliance?
- Who should I recruit as partners?
- What kind of an alliance should we create?

As you develop answers to these questions, you will find that you begin to look broadly at your own role in the community, your networks, and your ability to leverage resources. You will ensure that the vision of your organization remains in tune with the needs of the community or the individuals you serve, because the more partnerships you form, the more you are interconnected with the community.

As consultants, we have traveled around the country talking to nonprofit leaders about how to deal with cutbacks in funding. Through these discussions, we've learned that forming strategic alliances with other organizations has great potential to increase the resources and number of opportunities available to nonprofit leaders to accomplish their vision. Nonprofits are forming more alliances than ever before.

Our observations of successful alliances have generated some new ways of thinking about alliances. The majority of alliances formed by organizations are actually less intense and less complex than formal collaboration. They fall into the categories of what we call cooperation or coordination. These alliances have varying degrees of success, but all have the goal of generating more resources and delivering more impact than one organization can provide on its own.

Much work has been done on the most complex forms of alliances like collaboration and merger. Meanwhile, cooperation and coordination have not received the same amount of attention and are less understood. In business sector literature, however, alliances of all forms are much more extensively studied and promoted as "prime vehicles for future growth" and "incredibly, even decisively, important."[1]

> **We believe there is an increasing need for nonprofits to understand and strategically form alliances that work at a lower level of intensity and work well for all partners.**

We believe there is an increasing need for nonprofits to understand and strategically form alliances that work at a lower level of intensity and work well for all partners. Leaders form these less-intense alliances as logical responses to a range of external and internal pressures on their resources at a time when demands are as great as they have ever been.

This field guide draws on ideas in articles and books written for the business sector when we can see increased benefits to services and clients in the nonprofit sector. We hope that this guide helps you think differently about alliances and how to create them at the level of complexity that suits your goals—and no more. Perhaps those who have been hesitant to engage with others will use these ideas and processes to start a partnership that will strengthen their community.

The following section highlights five pressures facing nonprofits. You will undoubtedly have more factors that are particular to your community and organization, but the following factors will have a significant impact on all nonprofits for at least the next decade.

---

[1] Geoff Baum et al., "Introducing the New Value Creation Index," *Forbes ASAP* (April 3, 2000). http://www.forbes.com/asap/2000/0403/140.html. Also Charles Kalmbach Jr. and Charles Roussel, "Dispelling the Myths of Alliances," *Outlook Online* (Accenture Consulting, October 1999). http://www.accenture.com/xd/xd.asp?it=enweb&xd=ideas\outlook\special99\over_specialed_intro.xml.

## Pressures to Form Alliances

Leaders in the nonprofit sector are dealing with an ever-increasing number of forces in the environment that pressure organizations to form alliances with others. While there are a multitude of factors at play, five key items in the environment make forming alliances with others a critical skill for all nonprofits:

1. Pressure to do more with less

2. Scrutiny of nonprofits

3. Duplication of services seen as wasteful

4. Large-scale challenges require large-scale solutions

5. Increasing complexity of issues and solutions

### 1. Pressure to do more with less

First, nonprofits face increased pressure to do more with less. Many people have called the current environment "the perfect storm" because as revenue from all the main income sources for nonprofits declines, the demand for nonprofit programs and services has never been greater. Federal, state, and local governments are committed to holding the line on or reducing the dollars in their contracts and grants to nonprofits. Simultaneously, foundations, corporations, and individuals are experiencing an economy that has been through a recession and the related decline in assets. Communities, families, and individuals look toward nonprofits to meet more and more of their needs.

The "perfect storm"

Labeling this pressure as the perfect storm is poetic and draws attention to the problems nonprofits face, but does a disservice to the scale of the situation. This is more of a global climate change than a storm that will pass. These pressures have been present—and increasing—for two decades through both conservative and liberal policy swings. Therefore, businesses and organizations are changing the way they work together to "make lemonade." Nonprofits, in particular, are using this climate as a springboard to bring together multisector and interdisciplinary partners in innovative alliances that create stronger, healthier communities and benefit clients and consumers with new and more effective programs and projects.

## 2. Scrutiny of nonprofits

Nonprofits face increased scrutiny from both inside and outside the sector. This closer inspection has been on the rise for ten to fifteen years, spurred on by scandals in the for-profit sector and periodic misuse of funds by nonprofits. In response, nonprofits are beginning to focus on measuring the effectiveness of their services or contributions to the community by articulating and quantifying their outcomes and being more conversant with indicators and benchmarks. Sophisticated consumers are also demanding better quality in the services and products they receive. Alliances with strategically selected partners can bring increased positive visibility and credibility to organizations and attract potential funders.

## 3. Duplication of services seen as wasteful

Funders tend to view duplication of services as wasteful. When two or more organizations offer the same or similar services, funders may choose to support only one of the nonprofits. Funders increasingly ask community organizations to form alliances with larger multiservice organizations to play a bridging role between the service provider and its community members. This type of alliance allows multiservice organizations to offer services to people in communities they have not previously served and saves the effort and cost of building the capacity of each community-based organization to provide a whole range of services.

## 4. Large-scale challenges require large-scale solutions

Many funders and contractors are pushing for programs and projects to "go to scale." By this they are hypothesizing that to make a difference in certain community issues, size does matter. There is an assumption that efficiencies can be achieved and services made more effective by increasing the number of people who can be served and reducing the number of service providers. For many organizations the only way to bring a project to scale is by forming alliances with other organizations that significantly increase their resources, skills, and capacity.

## 5. Increasing complexity of issues and solutions

Nonprofits are trying to address increasingly complex issues and solutions, and no one organization has the required total expertise to best serve those needs. But each nonprofit has at least one core business at which it excels. Alliances among nonprofits with different core competencies help to address more complex problems. For example, nonprofits that form alliances with others can defray or spread the rising expense of research and development and obtain complementary resources and skills from partners. People are finding effective interdisciplinary approaches to solving complex community problems. Unprecedented alliances across professions and sectors can bring together a broad range of expertise to address comprehensive issues.

Clearly, nonprofits are gaining experience in forming alliances. Many of the nonprofits we have worked with have received at least one of the benefits listed in the next section through their alliances.

# Benefits (and Costs) of Alliances

Nonprofits intuitively seek the benefits offered by carefully conceived and managed alliances. These benefits include the ability to

1. Offer more and improved services to clients while using current or fewer resources

2. Gain access to new markets or communities

3. Attract additional, untapped revenue streams

4. Provide access to new technology or complementary skills

5. Increase the capacity to provide additional supplemental services that are more suited to the clients' needs

6. Reach out to people who are underserved or hard to serve

7. Provide the resources necessary to sustain research and development of new tools, processes, and services

8. Contribute to systems change through multisector alliances

## 1. Offer more and improved services to clients while using current or fewer resources

Alliances can truly allow nonprofits to do more with less, at least as compared to previous delivery modes. For example, a group of service providers came together to develop a contact list and map that detailed all services offered in the community for a target population. One of the organizations maintained this information on its web site with links to and from the other alliance members. In this way consumers had direct access to information that did not exist before, and the cost of access was kept to a minimum.

## 2. Gain access to new markets or communities

In nonprofit business, just as in for-profit business, market access is a key to success. Alliances give nonprofits access to different target populations that others serve, or help nonprofits connect with the customers of another organization who share a common interest in that organization's mission. For example, an organization providing congregate living to seniors served as a "bridge" to a recycling organization. The recycling nonprofit introduced recycling concepts to the residents who were unaware of the benefits of recycling. By becoming involved in recycling programs, the residents saved money and enjoyed using their new knowledge.

### 3. Attract additional, untapped revenue streams

Through alliances, organizations can create an array of programs or offerings impossible for one organization to provide alone. Creative blending of activities or brand-new programs may fit better within a funder's goals or have broader appeal to funders. For example, an organization that serves refugees and immigrants and a nonprofit providing employment services formed an alliance to request funding specifically designated for employment services for refugee and immigrant communities.

Use alliances to attract revenue

### 4. Provide access to new technology or complementary skills

Alliances can bring needed noncash resources—typically technology or skills—to partnering organizations. For example, a group of social service organizations formed an alliance around a program that required a web site. One of the organizations had staff who could design and maintain the web site. The alliance provided access for other participants to technical skills that none of them possessed.

### 5. Increase the capacity to provide additional supplemental services that are more suited to the clients' needs

Nonprofits often see needs among their clients that are related to their mission but just outside of it. Alliances can add value for their clients by adding the capacity to serve needs beyond those the individual nonprofit might normally address. For example, a nonprofit medical clinic formed an alliance with a mental health organization and a dental clinic to provide a range of screening services at one drop-in site. The result was a more efficient, effective way to meet the clients' needs.

### 6. Reach out to people who are underserved or hard to serve

Some of our most ingrained social problems occur among populations that are difficult to serve. Alliances can link programs having high client access with programs that offer needed services. For example, through its neighborhood leadership program, an organization in St. Paul, Minnesota, increases grassroots leaders' ability to provide leadership in their community. The leadership program targets a single neighborhood in St. Paul each year and forms an alliance with a neighborhood-based organization to help promote the program, serve as the site for the program, and fundraise for the program. In 2004, the program was offered in a community with a large number of Spanish and Hmong speakers. The partnering organizations created a pool of trained interpreters to translate for the program's participants and to be an ongoing resource for neighborhood meetings and events.

### 7. Provide the resources necessary to sustain research and development of new tools, processes, and services

Needs seem to be increasing in complexity, whether because society is more complex or because growing sophistication makes us more aware of the complexity of problems. Either way, the demands on organizations for better, more complex approaches typically outstrip the time and money the organizations have to improve services. Alliances can resolve this problem efficiently by pooling resources to sustain research and develop new tools, processes, and services.

**Each organization must determine for itself how much control it is willing to give up for this opportunity to gain resources.**

### 8. Contribute to systems change through multisector alliances

One of the biggest influences on an organization's ability to form and succeed at alliances is the mind-set of the organization's leadership. Faced with problems and under pressure to address these problems quickly, many nonprofit leaders tend to develop solutions in isolation rather than discuss them with others. When thinking through strategies for addressing problems or opportunities, some leaders assume that their boundaries for making change are confined to what they can control and directly affect. For most leaders, this control translates into decisions about the organization's assets (budget, staff and volunteers, building and property) and the less tangible but very real assets of relationships with stakeholders. Many leaders guard these assets carefully.

When leaders want to have a larger impact on accomplishing the organization's mission, they must change the course of discussion in the organization and with community members from How do we, in our nonprofit organization, solve the problem of increasing need and declining resources? to How do we, the community, address this problem? This is a shift from perceiving the problem as being solely the organization's concern to being the partners' and, indeed, the entire community's concern. This is also a shift in the amount of control of outcomes that individual leaders can have. By drawing the boundaries loosely around an organization, leaders can expand their thinking about available resources. Rather than focusing solely on individual budgets, they can look to the entire community and invite others to own and take credit for accomplishing some of the vision's elements. Although it is too simplistic to say a direct link exists between releasing control and gaining more resources, each organization must determine for itself how much control it is willing to give up for this opportunity to gain resources.

Such benefits are not without costs. Forming complex alliances is an expensive strategy that many nonprofits find hard to initiate and sustain. Included in the costs of forming alliances are

- Loss of resources. Alliances require planning and lots of meetings—which eat up staff time and resources.

- Slow start-up. Project start-up time tends to be longer because of a shared decision-making process involving several organizations. Short term, there is a loss of service delivery.

- Loss of control. Alliances, by definition, require sharing. Organizations in alliances typically lose some control of project outcomes, as outcomes may depend on other organizations' staff without any way to hold them directly accountable.

- Risk to reputation. Blame as well as credit and the risks as well as the rewards are shared with others.

- Loss of opportunity. The ability and flexibility to respond to other opportunities are restricted because scarce resources are committed to partners in a long-term project.

When leaders consider an alliance, they must weigh the benefits and costs for their organization and the community they serve.

## Who This Book Is For

This field guide is written to help nonprofit executive directors, managers, board members, and consultants make certain that resources are spent wisely and to help you understand how different kinds of alliances can do that.

Because funders often request (or mandate) some form of alliance, this field guide is for funders as well. It will help you have a more complete understanding of the different kinds of partnerships that can be formed and the results that can be achieved in each form of alliance.

Nonprofit leaders and funders will learn to think about and form alliances in new ways—expanding the possibilities for responding to opportunities and problems. This field guide provides practical worksheets and troubleshooting advice for all those who want to improve their current alliances and begin forming promising new ones.

## How to Use This Field Guide

This field guide will help you

- Explore elements of effective alliances and understand the wide range of ways that you can engage with others
- Identify action steps you can take to plan or start an alliance
- Discover ways to strengthen a current alliance

Chapter 1 helps you understand what alliances are and describes in detail the neglected, but often best-choice forms of alliance (cooperation and co-ordination). Chapter 2 provides a set of steps you can follow to (1) decide whether an alliance will help achieve the outcomes you desire, (2) find the right partners, (3) form the type of alliance(s) that will best achieve your goals, (4) formalize the structure of the alliance, and (5) manage the ongoing alliance. Chapter 3 is an in-depth look at two problems that often derail alliances—a mismatched structure or relationship difficulties among the partners. The appendixes include worksheets, samples, and a resource list to help you learn more about alliances.

We encourage you to use the sections of this book that best meet your needs.

# 1. Understanding Alliances

Every day nonprofits agree to partner with others—nonprofit, for-profit, and government—to better meet their mission during times of tight resources. They do so with varying degrees of logic and success.

We believe alliances make good sense for nonprofits much of the time. As described in the Introduction, the benefits are many, chief among them being more impact for less effort. But success with alliances requires that they be used wisely, and with a good understanding of which kinds of alliances will result in the best outcomes given the conditions and need.

## The Alliance Continuum: Terms We Use

While most, if not all, organizations work in partnership with others in some way, there is little agreement about the meaning of the words used to describe these partnerships. For example, people often use the terms *coordinate, cooperate,* and *collaborate* interchangeably in conversation and literature. In fact, there is significant confusion about what is meant by each word. So, let's start by defining the basic element of this discussion, the *alliance*:

> An alliance *is a relationship between partners that is strategically formed to accomplish goals that benefit the community while strengthening the partners.*

We'd better define partners as well:

> Partners *are two or more organizations that agree to work together on a mutually defined and implemented alliance.*

Throughout this field guide, we refer to a range of ways organizations can work together. Alliances fall into categories, or ranges, of intensity and complexity depending on the purpose for the alliance and the implementation strategies. We call this range an "alliance continuum." This continuum ranges from completely autonomous organizations on one end to merger on the other. (See Figure 1 below).

## Figure 1.  The Strategic Alliance Continuum

| Cooperation | Coordination | Collaboration | Merger |
|---|---|---|---|
| Less | Complexity and Intensity | | More |

We use the following definitions that were first framed in Winer and Ray's *Collaboration Handbook* and La Piana's *Nonprofit Mergers Workbook* to refer to the different types of alliances:

**Cooperation:** Shorter-term informal relationships that exist without any clearly defined mission, structure, or planning effort.

**Coordination:** Longer-term, more formal relationships that rely on understanding of missions and focus on a specific effort or program.

**Collaboration:** More durable and pervasive relationships where participants bring separate organizations into a new structure with full commitment to a common mission.[2]

**Merger:** A partnership in which two or more corporations decide to become one.[3]

---

[2]  Michael Winer and Karen Ray, *Collaboration Handbook: Creating, Sustaining, and Enjoying the Journey* (Saint Paul, MN: Fieldstone Alliance, 1994), 22.

[3]  David La Piana, *The Nonprofit Mergers Workbook* (Saint Paul, MN: Fieldstone Alliance, 2000), 15.

Before they approach funders, alliance partners need to share a common understanding of the type of alliance that will be of greatest benefit to the community, clients, and the partnering organizations. Nonprofit organizations that respond to proposals or contracts are often unsure what level of partnering the funder or contracting agency expects and, therefore, find it difficult to determine the cost and level of effort needed. As a result, both funders and nonprofits are frustrated when it comes time to actually implement the grants. It makes sense to clarify up front what type of partnership is required so that organizations can decide whether (and how) to get involved. We encourage leaders of nonprofits to frame their conversations with partners and funders by explaining and using the terms above to develop a common understanding of what type of alliance is being considered.

Many resources, including the *Collaboration Handbook, Collaboration: What Makes It Work, The Nimble Collaboration,* and *The Nonprofit Mergers Workbook,* do an excellent job of describing collaboration and merger. We refer to these descriptions frequently in this field guide and recommend that anyone who is interested in pursuing a collaboration or merger consult these sources and others listed in the Bibliography. Funders who are interested in supporting interorganizational collaboration may find David La Piana's article, "Real Collaboration: A Guide for Grantmakers," of special interest.[4]

Most of this guide focuses on the less intense end of the alliance continuum—on forming and sustaining alliances that fall in the range of cooperation and coordination. These alliances require less planning and less complex implementation compared to collaboration or merger.

In the next section, we begin by distinguishing cooperation from coordination and discussing three specific areas—administrative functions, communications and advocacy, and service delivery—in which alliances can have a significant impact on an organization's efficiency and effectiveness.

---

[4] David La Piana, "Real Collaboration: A Guide for Grantmakers," a report written at the request of the Ford Foundation (January 2001). http://www.lapiana.org/research/real.html.

## Cooperation, Coordination, and Collaboration

Factors that characterize an alliance as cooperation or coordination on the alliance continuum are related to the degree of intensity and the complexity involved in the alliance. Accordingly, alliances that are cooperative in nature are simpler to manage. They tend to be narrow in scope, and the partners remain independent at all levels of the partnership. While less demanding than more intense forms, these alliances typically yield fewer long-term benefits for the partnering organizations. At mid-range of the continuum, partners coordinate to capitalize on different capabilities of each partner and involve dedicated staff time. Figure 2, page 17, taken from the book *Collaboration: What Makes It Work,* clarifies the differences and unique elements of cooperation and coordination and compares them to collaboration. We encourage you to refer to this table as you begin to think about what kind of alliance would most benefit your organization.

For some organizations, the less intense types of alliances can be stepping-stones to more complex alliances. Partners can progress from cooperation to coordination and sometimes to collaboration. Those who have worked together successfully on a small project in the past will be more likely to enter into an alliance on a larger, riskier, and more complex project because of the previous positive experience. A project that starts as a simple one may become more complex as partners gain confidence in the alliance and see increased opportunity to accomplish mutual goals.

Here's an example of three organizations that increased the complexity of their alliance after developing trust. Three homeless shelters served some of the same homeless people in a city. The staff of these shelters had been in a low-intensity alliance, meeting regularly for many years to share information about their respective supporting services so they could encourage clients to participate in the programming that best met clients' needs. Over time, the organizations' staff developed a good working relationship and a high level of mutual trust. One of the shelters wanted to provide employment counseling to unemployed guests. However, the shelter could not afford to hire an employment counselor, nor did it have enough guests to constitute a full caseload. Staff of this shelter approached the other two

## Figure 2.  Cooperation, Coordination, and Collaboration Table[5]

| Essential Elements | Cooperation | Coordination | Collaboration |
|---|---|---|---|
| Vision and Relationships | • Basis for relationship is usually between individuals but may be mandated by a third party<br>• Organizational values are a common element<br>• Interaction is on an "as needed" basis, may last indefinitely | • Individual relationships are supported by the organizations they represent<br>• Missions and goals of the individual organizations are reviewed for compatibility<br>• Interaction is usually around one specific project or task of definable length | • Commitment of the organizations and their leaders is fully behind their representatives<br>• Creates common, new mission and goals<br>• Undertakes one or more projects for longer-term results |
| Structure, Responsibilities, and Communication | • Relationships are informal; each organization functions separately<br>• No joint planning is required<br>• Conveys information as needed | • Organizations involved take on needed roles, but function relatively independently of each other<br>• Requires some project-specific planning<br>• Establishes communication roles and creates definite channels for interaction | • Creates new organizational structure and/or clearly defined and interrelated roles that constitute a formal division of labor<br>• Requires more comprehensive planning that includes developing joint strategies and measuring success in terms of impact on the needs of those served<br>• Beyond communication roles and channels for interaction, creates many "levels" of communication as clear information is a keystone of success |
| Authority and Accountability | • Leadership is unilateral and control is central<br>• All authority and accountability rests with the individual organization, which acts independently | • Some sharing of leadership and control<br>• Some sharing of risk, but most of the authority and accountability falls to the individual organizations | • Authority is determined by the collaboration to balance the individual organizations' ownership with expediency to accomplish purpose<br>• Disperses leadership and mutually shares control<br>• All organizations in the collaboration share risk equally |
| Resources and Rewards | • Resources (staff time, dollars, and capabilities) are separate, serving the individual organization's needs | • Resources are acknowledged and can be made available to others for a specific project<br>• Rewards are mutually acknowledged | • Resources are pooled or jointly secured for a longer-term effort that is managed by the collaborative structure<br>• Organizations share in the products; more is accomplished jointly than could have been individually |

5   From Paul W. Mattissich, Marta Murray-Close, and Barbara Monsey, *Collaboration: What Makes It Work,* 2nd ed. (Saint Paul, MN: Fieldstone Alliance, 2001), 61. Originally adapted from the works of Martin Blank, Sharon Kagan, Atelia Melaville, and Karen Ray. Used with permission.

shelters about pooling enough resources to hire a counselor, develop a curriculum, and provide the service to the guests at all three shelters. After some discussion about budgets and facility use, the three shelters decided to deepen their alliance to implement this project. In this way the alliance achieved an economy of scale and the shelters were able to jointly support one counselor.

**Most small nonprofits can be part of only one or two significant alliances at a time given the amount of time and energy that these structures require.**

For most organizations, it makes sense to form the least complex alliance possible and still get the job done. Most small nonprofits can be part of only one or two significant alliances at a time given the amount of time and energy that these structures require. If an organization's leadership spreads itself too thin, it will not be able to accomplish the organization's most important work, even in the right alliances. Too often organizations create alliance structures that are more complex than necessary to accomplish the goals of the project. For instance, it is tempting to include legislators or funders as partners despite having no active role for them to play in the alliance. Or an alliance may structure itself after another successful model without considering that their goals are not the same. The result is that time and resources are spent unnecessarily to support a complex structure and decision-making process, leaving less time and resources available for participating in other alliances.

### Conditions for cooperation, coordination, or collaboration

So how do nonprofit leaders know what type of alliance would best fit their need or idea?

We'll start with the simplest form of alliance, cooperation. The following conditions suggest **cooperation** with your partners:

- Exchanging information is all that each of the partnering organizations expects.
- A funder or government agency raises the concern that two or more organizations are unaware of what is happening in their mutual areas of interest.
- A funder or government agency perceives a duplication of services.

- Cooperation rewards all participating organizations equally.
- Customers or clients participate in the programming of all potential allies and will directly benefit from the shared information.

For example, two organizations with similar missions noticed that individual donor support had dramatically decreased due to the slowing economy. Donor support was critical to keeping their advocacy staff present at the state capitol, but cuts in donations caused them to reduce the amount of time staff spent following bills through committees—something critical to both organizations' missions. When staff from the two organizations realized they were facing similar risks to their mission, they formed an alliance to monitor bills in different committees, thus reducing duplication of advocates. Hourly, daily, or as needed, the remaining staff exchanged information about the progress of bills. In addition, they purchased pagers and notified each other of the need for testimony or other personal presence. By exchanging information in this way, each organization continued to monitor the same number of bills with fewer staff.

The following conditions suggest **coordination** with your partners:

- Achieving economies of scale for a one-time event or short-term project.
- Agreeing on common outcomes or plans to be effective in the short-term.
- Sharing resources to best accomplish a short-term objective.
- Organizations need to maintain their individual identities within the context of the event or short-term project.

An example of coordination among partners involves several health and human service departments in a large urban county in the Midwest. To achieve efficiencies in administrative support of boards and to better coordinate the activities of the health and human services departments, a health and human services board was formed to develop and approve a plan and budget for both the public health department and the social services department. The result of this alliance is that the departments, while remaining distinct within the county, provide a more coordinated and efficient delivery of services. In addition, advisory groups have been formed to provide input from the county's residents into the planning process. This coordinated approach made it easier for elected officials to receive a unified funding request from both departments, which in turn led to greater funding for the departments.

The following conditions suggest **collaboration**[6] with your partners:

- The service system requires significant changes.
- To succeed, all or most of the players must be present.
- For sufficient impact, the issue must be addressed at a much larger scale and with many more resources than any one organization can muster.
- The challenge is complex and requires long-term, multiparty commitment.

For example, a nonprofit organization that serves people with developmental disabilities wanted to determine the best way to offer and improve a special-needs parenting service it provided for low-income people. However, the nonprofit lacked the resources needed to evaluate its service, and could not secure funding for evaluation. In the same community, a college with a social service program wanted to find a site for its interns each quarter. The educational institution formed an alliance with the nonprofit that benefited them both. The interns got excellent experience evaluating the results of the service over a long period of time, the nonprofit used the results to improve its services, and the college saved the time and expense of finding a new site for its interns each quarter.

As you and your leadership team discuss the assets and needs of your organization, you will develop an idea of what type of alliance would work best for your needs. You will also better understand what specific project you want to propose to partners. In the following section, we give specific examples of alliances in three key areas where organizations face the greatest opportunities and problems.

---

[6] While this work does not focus on collaboration, an understanding of its conditions will help you picture the continuum.

# Forming Alliances to Address Strategic Gaps

Each alliance that an organization forms must address a strategic gap in resources, skills, connections—whatever the organization has identified as a barrier to achieving its mission. As the complexity of a problem or opportunity increases (and often its impact on the organization), the intensity of the partnership also increases. The trick is creating an alliance in which intensity of the partnership matches the complexity of the need.

By *intensity of the partnership,* we mean the level of involvement and interconnectedness among partners, usually expressed via the relationships developed around shared finance, service delivery, or infrastructure. By complexity of the need, we refer to the number of variables that have an impact on the desired outcome—that is, more complex outcomes usually have many more inputs and many more risks. It is a balancing act. When assembling an alliance, you don't want to create relationships that require more work than the desired outcome needs—you don't want to waste staff time or money on needless meetings, policies, and so forth. At the same time, a complex outcome will likely require many types of resources and relationships. If you don't establish an alliance with relationships, policies, finances, and so forth at a level that will deliver the outcome, you've set up the alliance to fail.

We have identified three areas in an organization where an alliance with the right partner can have the greatest impact: 1) administration, 2) communications and advocacy, and 3) service delivery.[7]

1. For our purposes, *administration* refers to the traditional administrative activities that are necessary for the operation of every nonprofit (record keeping, fundraising, management systems, and so forth). These activities typically do not include direct interaction with customers or clients.

2. *Communications and advocacy* refers to both information sharing among partners and external communication to constituents, including funding proposals, policy statements, media relations, and promotional efforts directed toward clients and the general public.

---

[7] Thanks to Carol Lukas of the Fieldstone Alliance for originally noting the importance and relationship of these three areas in alliances. Carol has authored several books including *Consulting with Nonprofits, Conducting Community Forums,* and *Strengthening Nonprofit Performance: A Funder's Guide to Capacity Building.*

3. *Service delivery* involves the activities related to serving clients, including intermediary roles such as case management, intake, or technical assistance and capacity building.

Here are examples of cooperation, coordination, and collaboration in each of the three specific areas. Charts that clarify the relationship between the intensity of the alliance (from cooperation to collaboration) and the complexity of the project or situation follow the examples.

## 1. Administration

Administrative alliances are somewhat easier to form and maintain than those in communications or service delivery. For the most part, clients do not see administrative functions. An administrative alliance's main impact is most often behind the scenes, strengthening organizations' infrastructure.

An example of how organizations might *cooperate* in the administration area includes distributing information and materials on topics of interest to clients of both organizations. A case in point involves five intermediary organizations that regularly met to share information about their work, new programming, and conferences and workshops they were putting on. These meetings enabled the participating organizations to avoid duplication and, where possible, support each other's work by making referrals or cosponsoring an activity. In another example of administrative cooperation, a local college annually sponsors a student-run demographic study of the community. The college shares the study's results with all local nonprofits to help them better understand the community's growth and needs.

Moving up the scale to *coordination* (a higher degree of complexity), smaller nonprofits can see significant savings in sharing staff, such as a temporary bookkeeper or grant writer, with other small nonprofits. Many organizations are beginning to colocate or sublease office space from one lead organization, as in the case of the three organizations that share common meeting space in a building where each has offices. Only one of the organizations leases the meeting space; however, the other two organizations pay a monthly fee to help cover the cost of the lease. In another example of administrative coordination, an organization offers services in small private offices during the day and shares its space and phones with another organization at night. This second organization has volunteers who use the phones to solicit membership contributions.

If partners are ready to move beyond cooperation and coordination to *collaboration,* many find that developing a centralized purchasing program or pooling for better health insurance benefits creates savings for all participants. Figure 3 suggests alliances that can have significant impact for partners in the administration area.

### Figure 3.  Alliances to Improve Administration

| | |
|---|---|
| **Collaboration** | • Centralized purchasing or benefits programs<br>• Fiscal agent or sponsor for a project with joint staff<br>• On-site administration of a jointly provided service |
| **Coordination** | • Colocation of staff<br>• Shared temporary staff (bookkeeper, grant writer)<br>• Shared equipment |
| **Cooperation** | • Joint board and staff development<br>• Information distribution to customers or clients<br>• Sharing survey or study results |

*Increasing Intensity* ↑

Increasing complexity and impact →

## 2. Communications and advocacy

The second area where alliances can be beneficial to organizations is in communications and advocacy, or community connections. This broad area includes sharing information among partners, public awareness campaigns, legislative and executive lobbying and advocacy, educating funders, and fundraising.

An example of *cooperation* in communications: The managers of two training organizations regularly meet to exchange information and training schedules, which helps them avoid duplication of topic matter or planning important events for the same date. This enables customers to participate in each organization's trainings. Another example involves twenty-two organizations working in affordable housing, employment, parole transition, and other social services throughout seven rural counties. These organizations formed a cooperative to share information on the location of their services. The organizations decided to compile and maintain a map for clients. Updated quarterly, the map is available at every service site and informs clients of how and where to access the most appropriate and convenient services. Monthly meetings help the cooperating organizations share information about changes in the service population.

An example of *coordinating* in the area of communications: Many organizations form a short-term communications alliance with others in their field to advocate for the passage of a bill or to raise the awareness of the impact of pending legislation.

An example of *collaborating* in the area of communications: With increasing pressures from funders and others to work together, many nonprofits are writing packaged funding requests and leveraging their collaborative relationship to access new funding streams. In one case, five refugee and immigrant organizations jointly wrote a grant to get capacity-building support for their organizations. In the process of writing for this grant, they discovered ways to achieve economies of scale and included these ideas in their application. The funder wanted to support their working together and, therefore, funded one of the organizations as the fiscal sponsor for the collaboration.

Figure 4 suggests alliances that can have a significant impact for partners in the area of communications and advocacy.

**Figure 4.  Alliances to Improve Communications and Advocacy**

| | |
|---|---|
| **Collaboration** | • Packaged funding requests<br>• New funding streams |
| **Coordination** | • Advocacy on policy issues (welfare reform, community violence)<br>• Cosponser community forums |
| **Cooperation** | • Sharing advertising expenses for arts performances<br>• Mapping program locations |

*Increasing Intensity* (vertical axis)

Increasing complexity and impact

## 3. Service delivery

Service delivery has long been an area where nonprofits immediately see the benefits of forming alliances. It is also an area that poses the greatest risk because it requires more integration of an organization's staff and volunteers and affords less control over outcomes and reputation. These alliances affect when and how programs and services are provided. The most effective alliances help reduce duplication of services and increase the reach and professionalism of the program provided. Cooperative alliances range from sharing promising practice information to sharing customers (for instance, homeless shelters often serve the same people on different nights). Staff of several organizations that provide similar services in different geographic regions might attend joint training on best practices or a technical aspect of the service.

Partners *coordinate* programming in many ways. Some arts organizations use a common service for selling tickets. Audience members need only call one number to purchase tickets for a range of performances. Some dance organizations share performance space to keep costs down. As another example, managers of two statewide organizations serving the developmentally disabled community meet several times a year to update an information and referral system that allows people with developmental disabilities to locate services. One of the organizations operates the information and referral system on an ongoing basis.

One idea that is gaining in attraction for many organizations is *coordinating* services, sometimes called the "mall approach" to addressing common client needs. An example of the mall approach entails three organizations that formed an alliance to provide housing services, employment services, and access to education for people without a high school diploma. They operated the program out of a community center. The alliance provided a good mix of services and supports for clients with multiple needs.

At the most intense form of alliance, organizations *collaborate* to make a larger impact on a service or a system than they could make alone. Some examples: Three organizations jointly hired an intake person to process new clients and decide which of the three organizations should serve each client. Two organizations—one that provides chemical dependency treatment and the other transitional living—formed an alliance to jointly employ a case manager. The case manager works with clients that need both kinds of service to be successful. Five metropolitan health care providers realized that they shared many clients. These providers originally got together to create a uniform intake form; however, they soon realized that they wanted to meet and rethink their service delivery system to make it seamless. They agreed to form a partnership to develop common intake practices, a common set of services, a common referral system, and a common fee structure.

Figure 5 suggests alliances that can have significant impact for partners in the service delivery area.

**Figure 5.  Alliances to Improve Service Delivery**

| | |
|---|---|
| **Collaboration** | • Seamless service delivery system<br>• Shared staff (intake person, case manager)<br>• Services provided in new ways |
| **Coordination** | • Creating a common intake form<br>• Joint support of an information and referral system<br>• "Mall approach" to addressing the needs of shared clients |
| **Cooperation** | • Providing best practice information on a specific program model<br>• Sharing customer and audience information |

*Increasing Intensity* (vertical axis label)

Increasing complexity and impact

# Summary

This chapter provides a framework for understanding a range of alliances and gives examples of three areas where alliances have been beneficial. We hope this model helps you think more clearly about the alliances you may already be involved in (most nonprofits do some level of cooperation now and then) as well as imagine new ones that will enhance your ability to achieve your mission. In the next chapter, we outline a five-step process to strategically develop alliances that make the best use of resources and attract the right partners.

# 2. Forming Alliances

Our review of the literature on alliances revealed many processes for forming them, some with as few as three steps and some with eight or more. Some authors focus on managing the relationships among alliance partners and others focus on maximizing measurable results. In this chapter, we suggest a five-step process to create and implement an alliance that balances personal relationships and organizational imperatives.

The process of forming an alliance usually begins in one of two ways. Sometimes one person develops a good idea based on his or her experiences and on an intuitive understanding of emerging challenges or opportunities. At other times, two or more leaders brainstorm an idea in a meeting or over lunch that tackles joint problems or emerging opportunities.

To harness the energy and excitement around this new idea, it is important to gather a team to help move the process from a "good idea" to a more focused conversation. This team may consist of program managers, directors, or board members who think broadly and strategically about the assets and needs of the community and of the organization. The team evaluates how an alliance might address these assets and needs. If an alliance emerges as a strategy to pursue, the team considers who would be good partners. Next, the potential and committed partners complete the planning, and structure and formalize the alliance. Finally, the partners agree on how to manage and implement the alliance.

To further explain the activities in each step, we will use a running example of an alliance formed by two organizations that enabled each to better respond to the needs of the community, gain access to new funding, and more successfully achieve their mission.

## Steps in Forming an Alliance

There are five steps to forming an alliance. Steps 1 and 2 happen without partners, as the organization identifies gaps and considers potential allies. Steps 3 through 5 happen in cooperation with potential or chosen allies. We've presented the steps linearly, but, as with all processes that involve people, actual events are often iterative and circular in nature. Some people may follow the steps as presented, but others may need to reorder or skip steps to match their unique circumstances. It may be necessary to revisit steps to ensure buy-in from all partners.

The worksheets found Appendix A have questions designed to help you address a variety of situations. We encourage you to tailor the process to your unique needs, using only the worksheets that are helpful to you. The five basic steps of forming an alliance are

1. **Clarify the purpose**
   Determine the needs of your organization and your community. This work often results in a brief concept paper that is used in discussion with potential partners.

2. **Identify and recruit partners**
   Using the concept paper, identify and meet individually with potential partners to determine who shares your interest in the project outcomes.

3. **Frame the alliance**
   Partners commit to the project and begin to plan the project.

4. **Formalize the structure and plan**
   Partners jointly develop a detailed plan, budget, and structure for the alliance and formalize it in a written agreement.

5. **Implement and manage the alliance**
   Partners implement the alliance and share leadership and ownership.

Let's look at these steps in detail.

## Figure 6.  The Process of Forming an Alliance

| Purpose of step | Who is responsible | Time frame | Outcome | Products | Worksheet(s) |
|---|---|---|---|---|---|
| **Step 1**<br>Clarify the purpose | Initiating organization | • One or two brainstorming sessions | You decide that an alliance with others will help further your mission | • Concept paper | 1, 2 |
| **Step 2**<br>Identify and recruit partners | Initiating organization | • One brainstorming session<br>• Time needed to recruit partners | The initial idea attracts additional partners and is reframed through discussion | • List of possible partners<br>• Recruitment plan | 3, 4 |
| **Step 3**<br>Frame the alliance | Potential and committed partners | • One or two meetings of the partners<br>• Writing time | Potential and current partners develop a commitment to an alliance with specific goals | • Revised concept paper—with kind of alliance<br>• List of additional potential partners | 4 |
| **Step 4**<br>Formalize the structure and plan | Committed partners | • One to three meetings<br>• Writing time | Partner agreements are formalized in a written form | • Memo of understanding | 5 |
| **Step 5**<br>Implement and manage the alliance | Committed partners | • Regular, ongoing meetings | Partners develop a work plan and begin to implement the alliance project | • Work plan | |

# Step 1:  Clarify the Purpose

Some leaders think it is a luxury to take the time to think strategically about forming partnerships. Those who treat strategic thinking as a necessity rather than a luxury will find the time well spent. These leaders are better able to be flexible when faced with unexpected opportunities and can react quickly to crises. Find opportunities to regularly examine how your organization's skills and unique capabilities align with its objectives, strategies, budget, and plans. Evaluate your programming outcomes and determine whether your community or organization has needs that you cannot meet with the resources available to you. One way to ensure that such planning happens regularly is to include partnership considerations in your organization's annual strategic planning process.

Use alliances to create a bigger "resource pie"!

Partnerships can be grounded in the kind of exciting and energizing planning described earlier. But executive directors are often persuaded (or, to put it more bluntly, coerced) to think about alliances (especially collaboration) by funders, regulating agencies, or other outside forces. Many funders now create requests for proposals that are open *only* to organizations that apply jointly—with ideas that promote economies of scale, broader and more diverse community involvement, greater client access to services, and reduced duplication of effort. Such pressure can be good or bad.

Often money or staff time—your key resources—are the drivers for partnerships. Most organizations believe there's only so much resource "pie" to be divided. This belief weighs heavily on discussions of what is needed to turn a vision into reality. Rather than restricting your organization to what it must "give up" to gain a partner, our experience tells us it's better to think beyond a vision of a static, limited amount of resources. Instead, imagine creating a bigger pie. Think about how to access greater opportunities and new funding sources.

Whether alliance ideas emerge from your organization or from an outside entity, you must determine if the purpose of the suggested alliance truly fits with your mission and vision for the future. In other words, you need to be clear on how an alliance can serve your organization's self-interest before committing time and resources to it. Note that your organization's self-interest is grounded in meeting the needs and interests of your clients and community.

In her article, "Understanding Successful Partnerships and Collaborations,"[8] Katherine James suggests that, as you begin to think about forming alliances, you consider these two questions:

1. If we only had _____, we could _____.

2. What do we have to offer a partner?

For Step 1, gather a group of people who have a good understanding of your organization's strengths and weaknesses—usually your leadership team—to

---

[8] Katherine James, "Understanding Successful Partnerships and Collaborations," *Parks and Recreation* (May 1999): 41.

begin the conversation on the first question, *If we only had _____,*
*we could _____.* Keep the conversation at the wide-open, brainstorm
level at first; every idea is a good one.

At times, the answer to this question will be self-evident. It may be a logical continuation of a long-standing conversation on a critical issue for the
organization, or the team may realize that new opportunities or changes in
the environment make this a good time to form new alliances.

At other times, the answer to the question will take longer to derive. Answers could be "If we only had Spanish-speaking staff, we could offer our
clinic's services in the local Hispanic community," or "If we only had another basketball court, we could set up a basketball league for the youth in
our community." To move the discussion forward, you can analyze your
organization's service gaps or duplications relative to its mission (*service
delivery*), the changing external environment (*external environment*), or
your organizational capacity (*internal capacity*).

Use the following questions to jumpstart ideas in the conversation:

### Service delivery

- Are there some desired outcomes that we have been unable to achieve
  on our own?
- Are there strategies that we would like to implement but need more
  resources?

### External environment

- Is system-wide advocacy important for accomplishing our mission?
- Do we want to change the way the system operates? If so, how?

### Internal capacity

- What are the key values in our organization?
- How much of our resources can we devote to the alliance without jeop-
  ardizing other areas of our programming?
- Are there some administrative services that we need but cannot afford?

Worksheet 1: Clarify the Purpose of the Alliance, pages 72–73, can help you frame this discussion. As you develop answers for these questions, you may find that forming alliances is a good way to gather the resources or influence necessary for your needs.

After holding the conversations with your leadership team, solidify your ideas in a brief, written concept paper. This is an initial version of the concept paper that you are drafting. As you progress through the next steps, you will be adding to and changing the concept paper to reflect the ideas and needs of your partners. By the time you get through Steps 4 and 5, you will have a much more detailed concept with precise outcomes.

For this initial version of the concept paper, outlining your ideas in writing helps to clarify the options you will discuss with others. The concept paper can be used in discussions with potential partners, funders, advisors, and others as a way to quickly convey a picture of the alliance and its impact. It needs to give potential partners a general idea of the alliance that you are asking them to join, but also allow them to reshape or modify the goals and the strategies to ensure that their needs are also met. By helping to create the vision for the alliance, partners become engaged. Therefore, the initial concept paper should include

- A brief discussion of the *history* that led to this strategy or alliance idea.

- The *purpose of the proposed alliance:* What good is to be accomplished, and for whom?

- Two or three key *outcomes:* What do you hope will be different in the future because of the alliance?

- A brief *outline* of the first steps to get the alliance started, including how the outcomes will be achieved, the scale or scope of the effort (described in terms of time frame, numbers of clients affected, number of partners desired, or other parameters).

Worksheet 2: Develop the Concept Paper, pages 74–75, includes questions to help you draft a concept paper. A sample concept paper can be found in Appendix B, page 86.

Try not to make any decisions about forming partnerships until you reflect on the full range of alliance options and determine which type would be best in your particular situation. Bring up names of organizations you could partner with only as *examples* of the types of help another organization could provide. By the end of this step you will decide whether or not to organize an alliance. If you decide to proceed with it, you will have a clear idea of what the alliance should accomplish, and are ready to begin identifying and recruiting partners.

---

### EXAMPLE

The ABC organization, located near Lincoln, Nebraska, is a nonprofit whose mission includes advocating for the rights of people with disabilities. As was his custom on January 1 every year, Johan, ABC's executive director, took the day to reflect on the strengths and needs of the organization—beginning with the phrase, If we only had_____, we could _____. As he reached his third cup of coffee, he decided that to be effective, he needed to involve young families in his organization. For the past few years young families with children with disabilities had not participated in ABC's advocacy programs. Instead, they joined a young parent's organization, XYZ, which had relevant information and programming, including support groups for young parents. In addition, LMN, a new, smaller nonprofit serving people with disabilities and their families successfully recruited families with children in elementary school because they had specific programming to help families with trouble in the school system.

Johan realized that to sufficiently influence policy makers to support a newly proposed school regulation, all of these parents needed to be involved in advocating for it. Johan wanted to get these young parents involved in the advocacy work of his organization, educated on the issue at hand, and willing to advocate with policy makers. Their involvement would give ABC's advocacy work the necessary, visible support of young families. While Johan would like to have young families involved in ABC's programs, he realized that it did not make sense to compete with XYZ and LMN's well-respected and cost-effective programming.

Johan continued his day of reflection on January 1 by considering what ABC could offer to potential partners. ABC is well respected for its strong advocacy program on a broad range of issues and could offer that expertise to other organizations. A "marriage" of connections and expertise could benefit all of the organizations and the people they serve. His reflection time complete, Johan was ready to act. He decided that after the holidays he would draft a brief concept paper outlining his thoughts and call a meeting of his management team to discuss the idea of forming an alliance with XYZ and LMN.

## Step 2: Identify and Recruit Partners

An alliance needs partners, so gather your leadership team together to begin identifying possible partners. Start by reviewing the concept paper developed in Step 1.

Once you and your leadership team decide what you want to accomplish with the help of partners, move to Katherine James's second question, What do we have to offer a partner? Each alliance must create win-win opportunities for all partners. Partners will not remain in alliances where their self-interest is not being met, or they feel they are providing an unfair share of the resources or work. Understanding what you have to offer that would interest another organization (and what you are willing to contribute to the alliance) is the foundation for identifying and attracting potential partners. Consider the following questions to start brainstorming.

### Service delivery

• Do we have unique services or programs?

### External environment

• Do we have a solid reputation in the community and with funders?
• Do we have special access to different sectors of our community—perhaps because of a special skill such as a bilingual staff or a refugee-run organization?

### Internal capacity

• Do we have an exceptional infrastructure, such as an accurate record-keeping and reporting system or an extraordinary marketing department?
• Do we have other resources we can share with others (for example, an excellent mailing list or a host of volunteers)?
• Do we have experience working in alliances with others?

Worksheet 3: What Do We Have to Offer a Partner, pages 76–77, can help you facilitate this discussion.

When you know what resources you can commit to an alliance, you might want to invite one or two potential partners to meet with you and your leadership team to help identify other organizations and individuals who might be interested in the concept and have something to offer the alliance. Until now, you and your team have been fully in control of the concept and working independently on the idea. With the next step, you will be working with others, allowing their ideas and needs to modify your original concept of the alliance. An open dialogue will bring out opportunities and new ways of working together. This openness and flexibility will ultimately give all partners widespread ownership in the alliance and will help make it a success. You might already have potential partners in mind as Johan did, or you might have successfully worked with an organization or two on a similar idea and want to see if they are interested in this one. Another way to identify potential partners is to brainstorm a list of organizations using the following questions:

- Who are leaders in our field of work?

- With whom have we worked before?

- Who are our competitors?

- With whom should we work for informational reasons or political reasons or both?

- Who has the skills, technical capabilities, or assets that we need and don't have?

The book *Collaboration: What Makes It Work* identifies twenty factors that help collaborations succeed; some of them are listed on the next page.[9] As you consider potential partners, use these factors as parameters to assist you in making the final decision of whom to invite.

---

[9] Mattessich, *Collaboration: What Makes It Work.*

Does the potential partner

- Share mutual respect, understanding, and trust with the other potential partners?
- See the alliance as vital to its self-interest?
- Show willingness to commit a senior leader who can accurately represent (and influence) his or her organization?
- Have a history in the community that shows the ability to compromise?
- Have a reputation in the community as a legitimate leader in the field?

Worksheet 4: Identify and Recruit Partners, pages 78–79, will help you identify a list of potential partners.

After creating a list of potential partners who might form the alliance and identifying what you can offer in return for their participation, decide who should invite each potential partner. This person should already have a relationship with the partner and, therefore, have the greatest likelihood of successful recruitment. In addition, the person who makes the call must be a champion for the concept. Suggest at least one date and time for the first meeting. Create a contact list to manage the recruitment process and format it in a way that identifies the key contact person and a deadline for approaching each partner. Schedule a meeting with each potential partner, share the alliance concept paper, and determine whether the organization shares an interest in the project outcomes. Ideally, the person you approach is someone who can make decisions on resource allocation for his or her organization. If the person does not have that kind of authority, be sure he or she can easily communicate with and request decisions from the decision makers. By the end of these invitation meetings, you will know who is willing to participate in the meeting of the potential partners.

In Step 3 you begin the exciting process by inviting your potential partners to a meeting to frame an alliance that includes everyone's ideas.

**EXAMPLE**

Johan's leadership team is really excited about his idea to expand ABC's advocacy for the new school regulation through an alliance with organizations that attract younger families. They agree that Johan and Carol, ABC's associate director, should brainstorm a list of potential partners for the alliance. In addition to the executive directors of XYZ and LMN, they list leaders from a local legal advocacy group called Legal Aid to Parents, a representative of the State Disability Office, and a program officer of Big Bucks Foundation who has supported ABC for many years. Johan and Carol divide up the list of potential partners and schedule visits with each of the leaders to present the alliance concept paper and discuss common interests. Four of the five leaders indicate interest in meeting to explore the concept of an alliance. The State Disability Office, while supporting the idea, does not want to be visible in the effort. The participants set a date to decide on goals and next steps.

## Step 3: Frame the Alliance

In this step, potential partners meet to decide whether to proceed with some form of alliance. You personally contacted each potential partner and now extend an invitation to attend a meeting with all the potential partners to discuss the concept.

At this meeting, you and your partners need to share self-interests, modify the ideas in the concept paper to craft a unified vision for the alliance, and generally determine how many resources will be necessary to proceed. Do this deliberately since, before this meeting, the initiator of the process is the only one who "owns" the vision in the concept paper. By the end of the meeting, all partners should have broad ownership in the alliance and the project.

If you gather people who can make decisions for their organization, you may end the first meeting with a decision from each person. Often, however, several participants will need to talk with others in their organization before making a decision. Some organizations may want to get clients' feedback or a community advisory group's reaction to the concept to discover how much support and interest there is before they commit their organization to the alliance. Such input can be gathered through a focus group or select phone or in-person interviews. In this case, end the meeting by agreeing on a process and a deadline for reaching a final decision as soon as possible. Potential partners may need to meet several times before deciding whether to go ahead with an alliance. New potential partners may be at each meeting, and some of the original attendees may decide that they cannot participate in the alliance. If all participants decide to stop exploring the concept, the process ends. Worksheet 5: Frame the Alliance, pages 80–81, will help you decide whether to proceed with any form of alliance.

However, if there are partners who think the alliance warrants further meeting time to implement the vision, the process continues. Once everyone states their intent, the committed participants must decide whether they have the partners needed to accomplish the goal of the alliance. If not, the group must discuss whether to recruit additional partners or reframe the concept to attract the required organizations to the table. Additional meetings may be needed to fully secure agreement from all necessary partners.

Make certain you identify *all* the necessary partners at this time. Here's why: After this step the group is starting to form. Establishing a core of partners at the start quickly brings stability to the alliance. Each time a new partner arrives, all participants have to review and recommit to the goals and outcomes. This is time consuming and frustrating for partners who are ready to act. The key words are *necessary partners*. Beware of including partners for purely political reasons. Each partner should have an active role and a stake in the outcomes of the alliance.

In summary, the outcomes for these meetings should include

- A written agreement on the goals and outcomes of the alliance and the difference the alliance will make in the community
- A list of partners who are committed to the alliance and their possible roles and responsibilities
- A list of other people who have an interest in what the alliance will do, including other potential partners
- A general idea of the resources the alliance will need, including those that committed partners can bring

- A decision about the type of alliance (cooperation, coordination, or collaboration), and its structure
- A draft work plan that outlines next steps
- A revised and expanded concept paper to share with additional potential partners

To obtain these outcomes from your alliance, the first meeting should

- Establish good relationships among participants. Take time at each meeting to get to know each other. Have each person state their names, the organization they represent, and why they are interested in the alliance concept.
- Hold an open and inclusive discussion on the alliance concept. Make sure everybody has a chance to ask questions, make suggestions, and modify the concept to fit their needs.
- Clarify who wants to be part of the alliance.
- Agree on how decisions will be made and determine what decisions are possible in these first meetings. Ideally the first decisions would be about
  - The kind of alliance (cooperation, coordination, or collaboration) and its structure
  - What role each partner will play and what resources each can contribute
- Consider adding partners and, if you decide to do so, identify who will recruit them.
- Conclude with an agreement on what the next steps are (including drafting and distributing a meeting summary and scheduling the next meeting date, time, and place) and identify who will accomplish them.

By the end of Step 3, you and your partners are prepared to flesh out the details of the alliance. Through your discussions, you now have a good idea about the alliance goals and partners and how to implement the alliance. Your initial concept has been modified but you have a clearer idea of what outcomes you can achieve and you have partners who are excited and committed to the alliance. In the next step, you and your partners will formalize those ideas in writing and incorporate the implementation details into a work plan.

**EXAMPLE**

At the first meeting to explore the alliance idea, Johan and the potential partners discuss the outcomes identified in the concept paper and expand on what they would like to see accomplished. Johan hired a consultant to facilitate this meeting so he can fully participate in the discussion. As the group brainstorms the idea, they add more goals: educating young parents on the roles of the respective organizations, on the workings of state agencies, on how regulations are developed, and on the importance of having effective regulations in place. By the end of the meeting, the leaders of ABC, XYZ, LMN, and Legal Aid to Parents commit to meet again to develop a plan and clarify any resources the alliance will need to meet its goals. The program officer from Big Bucks Foundation, while supportive, doesn't believe that the foundation should be part of the alliance. The remaining participants don't think that any other partners are needed in the alliance at this time and leave the meeting excited about the alliance's potential for making a difference in the lives of the young parents and their children.

## Step 4:  Formalize the Structure and Plan

In this step, you and your partners formalize a written agreement on the purpose, outcomes, general strategies, and if appropriate, resources needed for the alliance. This agreement expands both the content and detail of the initial concept paper used to interest and engage partners. Hammering out the details may take several meetings. This step prepares you and your partners for the implementation of the alliance. During this stage you will want to pull together some of the decisions that you made in Steps 1 through 3 and begin to address the details of the alliance. There are really two parts to this step. First, the partners should revisit and revise the initial concept paper. As you do so, you will uncover many issues and areas that need clarification. Second, the partners should draft a memo of understanding. Worksheet 6: Formalize the Structure and Plan for Success, pages 82–84, covers the concepts that you should work on during this step.

## Step 4A:  Revise the concept paper

The concept paper will become the basis for negotiating agreement among the partners. The best way to get that agreement is to systematically revisit and revise each part of the concept paper so that all partners are in agreement. While doing so, answer the following questions.

### The mission or purpose

What good will the alliance accomplish, and who will benefit? How does the purpose of the alliance relate to each partner's mission? Be sure the purpose statement describes your target population and any geographic parameters.

### Two to three key outcomes

What do you hope will be different in the future as a result of the alliance? Describe the outcomes from the perspective of your customers or clients and identify when these outcomes will be achieved.

### Strategies

How will the outcomes be achieved? The strategies should give a good idea of the broad approaches the alliance should use. Don't go into detail on the exact activities necessary to accomplish the strategies. The details are more appropriate in the implementation plan that you will create in Step 5.

### Known resources

What resources will the alliance need? Describe the resources necessary to implement the strategies. Consider funds, skills, knowledge, relationships, access to constituents or funds, communications—all the types of resources that may be required to accomplish your mission. To the extent possible, estimate and attach numbers (or other measurable description) to each of these needs.

### Partners

Who are the partners that are committed to this project? One last time consider whether anyone else should be at the table. Given what you have developed so far and your resource needs, determine whether you should try to recruit anyone else.

### Stakeholders

Who has an interest in the alliance's project? Who will be affected by its work? Who might provide resources? Who might be competing with you?

### Time frame

When will the project or program start? This date will help create a timeline for implementation planning. Consider how long it will take to raise the needed resources, establish systems and structure, and promote the project or program.

### Decision making

How will we make decisions related to the project? Which issues require all partners to be part of the decision and which can be delegated to one partner to decide unilaterally? Step 5 has an expanded discussion of this topic.

### Communication

How will formal and informal communication among partners happen? Who will take responsibility for maintaining a record of proceedings? Who will be the spokesperson with the public and key stakeholders?

After revisiting, expanding, and agreeing on these points in the concept paper, the partners need to address one more question—"showstoppers" or barriers to the successful implementation of the alliance.

**Showstoppers**

What might keep this alliance from happening? Identify barriers to getting the project off the ground (consider more than funding). Typical showstoppers might include opposition from the community or an inability to find the right site.

## Step 4B:  Draft a memo of understanding

Agreements that partners make as they complete the concept paper are typically detailed in a written form, usually called a memo of understanding, a letter of agreement, or a charter. This step is crucial for the success of the alliance. The level of intensity of the alliance determines the detail and specificity of the alliance's written agreement. The more intense the partnership and the more resources that are put at risk, the more detail is needed in the agreement. Figure 7, page 46, shows the items typically included in a memo of understanding for each type of alliance. For cooperation, since typically no funds are involved, a brief memo stating mutual expectations may be all that is necessary (see Appendix B, the sample memo of understanding on page 88). In a coordination, since there is a shared vision, work plan, and budget for a one-time event or a time-limited project, a more detailed agreement is needed (see Appendix B, the sample letter of agreement, page 89). Collaboration will require even more specificity on each item, particularly spelling out the length of commitment, accountability, and the amount of shared resources. (For additional examples of letters of agreement for a collaboration, consider samples in *The Nimble Collaboration*.)[10]

---

[10]   Karen Ray, *The Nimble Collaboration: Fine-Tuning Your Collaboration for Lasting Success* (Saint Paul, MN: Fieldstone Alliance, 2002).

**Figure 7: Items to Include in a Memo of Understanding**

| Item for memo of understanding | Cooperation | Coordination | Collaboration |
|---|:---:|:---:|:---:|
| Mission/purpose | X | X | X |
| Outcomes | X | X | X |
| Strategies | X | X | X |
| Resources | | X | X |
| Partners | X | X | X |
| Stakeholders | | X | X |
| Time frame | X | X | X |
| Decision making | | X | X |
| Communication | X | X | X |
| Competition | | | X |
| Conflict of Interest | | | X |
| Detailed work plan | | | X |

---

**EXAMPLE**

At the next two meetings of the alliance, the partners develop a letter of agreement that outlines a program (including a rough budget) that the alliance will operate. The outcomes of the program are to

- Recruit more young parents of disabled children from the programming of LMN and XYZ to actively advocate for the proposed school regulation.

- Provide a comprehensive training program for young parents so they understand the roles of each of the participating organizations, the background on the proposed regulation, and the regulation's probable impact on students.

- Involve the informed young parents in meetings the State Department of Education will hold on the regulation.

The ABC organization agrees to serve as fiscal sponsor for the project and to spearhead the advocacy effort. Legal Aid to Parents will provide training, and LMN and XYZ will recruit young parents to participate in the advocacy effort. The alliance decides that they will need $5,000 to defray the costs of marketing, training space, travel expenses, and child care. The leadership from each participating organization signs the following letter of agreement and the group is now ready to raise funds and implement the project.

Young Parents Involvement in School Regulation

**Alliance Letter of Agreement**

The Young Parents Involvement Project is a voluntary alliance among the following organizations:

- ABC
- LMN
- Legal Aid to Parents
- XYZ

These organizations all serve people with disabilities and their families. The purposes of this project are to

1. Recruit more young parents of disabled children from the programming of LMN and XYZ to actively advocate for the proposed school regulation.

2. Provide a comprehensive training program for young parents so they understand the roles of each of the participating organizations, the background on the proposed regulation, and the regulation's probable impact on students.

3. Involve the informed young parents in meetings the State Department of Education will hold on the regulation.

The alliance commits to

- Sharing information about the new school regulation
- Recruiting young parents into the project
- Providing training to young parents so that they can assist in revising the proposed school regulation
- Defraying the costs of parent involvement in the project

ABC will serve as the fiscal sponsor for the project and will take the lead in managing the advocacy component of the project.

LMN and XYZ will recruit young parents to participate in the project.

Legal Aid to Parents will provide training to help parents understand the issues involved in the proposed school regulation and enable them to effectively participate in the review and comment process.

*(continued)*

A budget of $5,000 is needed to implement the program as follows:

| Item | Amount | Use | Source |
|---|---|---|---|
| Recruitment brochures | $ 2,000 | Recruiting young parents | ABC |
| Meeting room | 500 | Training space | LMN |
| Travel expenses | 1,000 | Travel costs of parents and professionals | ABC |
| Child care | 1,500 | Care for children of parents during participation | XYZ |
| Total | $ 5,000 | | |

The alliance will strive to make all decisions by consensus; however, the fiscal sponsor is responsible for seeing that the grant is spent in accordance with the budget. We agree that the executive directors will represent their organizations and make every effort to attend every meeting. In the rare case that a director will be absent, the organization may appoint one alternate with voting rights.

Our organizations and the following representatives commit to participation in this project. (There will be separate signature blocks for all partners)

Authorized Signature: _____ Date: _____

Printed Name: _____ Title: _____

Organization: _____

# Step 5:  Implement and Manage the Alliance

Once the alliance is developed and the agreement signed, you will need to pay attention to two facets of the alliance. First, you need to implement the project or steps to accomplish the alliance's goals. Use your work plan and begin to take action. Until this point, alliance discussions typically involved the top leadership of the partnering organizations (or their designees). Now line staff from all the partners will be called on to implement the project and will need to develop relationships of trust and respect. The more complex the alliance, the more important it becomes to tend to these facets. In the case of a coordination or collaboration, a detailed work plan is needed. This work plan specifies who will do what in the next year—in other words, who is accountable for what outcomes of the project. In the situation of shared funds, a budget will also be needed.

Second, you need to manage the alliance—facilitate the meetings of partners and make joint decisions for the alliance. During the first few months of an alliance, all partners must build ownership in the alliance. Good facilitation of meetings and decision-making processes, accurate and complete communication with internal and external stakeholders, and leadership buy-in are critical. In the first meeting, partners must

- Agree on meeting facilitators
- Agree on a decision-making process
- Identify how communication will occur
- Keep an up-to-date work plan

Let's explore each of these in greater detail.

## Agree on meeting facilitators

There is power in the role of facilitator. Therefore, in the beginning of an alliance, it is often beneficial to either hire an outside facilitator or rotate the job of meeting facilitator among partners. The advantages to facilitation by an "outsider" are

- Each participant's voice can be heard
- No participant needs to focus on process
- Objective facilitation takes place, which enhances trust among the participants
- Group decisions occur more rapidly, so the project can begin sooner

Often an outside facilitator charges a fee, so some alliances include facilitation costs when applying for a small foundation grant to help with the start-up of the alliance. Facilitators may be located through web sites, professional directories, or word of mouth.

Some of these same outcomes may be achieved without the expense of hiring a facilitator by rotating leadership among the partners. Rotating the leadership promotes shared responsibilities and boosts ownership in the process. If partners handle the facilitation, it will be helpful to agree on expectations for the meetings, such as

- The facilitator (meeting chair) will draft a meeting agenda and distribute it with relevant attachments one week prior to the meeting
- Partners will make attending the meeting a priority and be prepared to discuss items on the agenda
- The facilitator will ensure that all participants get equal opportunity to express their thoughts
- Decisions will be made by consensus (see page 51) and recorded in the meeting minutes

## Agree on a decision-making process

Most alliances operate on a consensus basis; however, partners need to understand what is meant by consensus. Consensus does not mean that a proposed action needs unanimous support—it means that all members can live with the decision. We often describe consensus as reaching an agreement after hearing and discussing everyone's concerns. Consensus is about developing mutually acceptable decisions, creating group equality and ownership, understanding each other's issues, and exploring alternatives.

One simple process for reaching consensus involves discussing a topic or issue until one person clearly and concisely states a proposal (similar to stating a motion in the democratic process). The group then indicates whether they support the idea through voice approval, show of hands, or thumbs up or down. If someone disagrees with the idea, that person (and others around the table) need to modify the current idea or present an alternative for discussion. Often, group members will agree to support the proposal even if they are cautious or not entirely in favor of it because they have built up trust in the group and the project's outcomes to date. Record these decisions in the meeting notes so that the group can refer to them if questions arise in the future.

This is a very different mind-set from a democratic process where the self-interest of one organization is subjugated to the majority. However, in certain circumstances the democratic approach will benefit the alliance. Consensus decision making is time consuming, and some issues are either not important enough to warrant the time to reach consensus or are more time sensitive than others. The alliance should establish criteria for the type or level of decisions to make through a vote, to delegate to one of the partners to make unilaterally, or to make through consensus. Partners will not want to take meeting time to reach consensus on details like the color of curtains or type of paper used for printing, but you may want to reach consensus on purchasing a van or other high-cost items. When strong trust and relationships exist among partners, more decisions can be made through voting or delegation.

## Identify how communication will occur

Complete, accurate, inclusive communication is critical to any alliance. Consider the following communication channels when implementing an alliance project.

For both informal and formal *communication among the partners* related to alliance business, notify everyone of the date and time of meetings, recorded decisions, and updates on the alliance's progress.

For *communication with the public and stakeholders,* identify a spokesperson for funder contacts, media inquiries, public meetings, and customer or client messages. Different people can be identified for each role or audience; however, be clear on who can represent the alliance in different arenas. In addition, follow good message protocol (not a subject of this book): identify the key messages you want to give to each audience and stick to those messages.

For *communication with decision makers in partnering organizations,* the representative of each partnering organization should serve as the communication vehicle to the decision makers in their organization. In situations where the alliance formally requests something from partners, such communication needs to be in the form of a written proposal or memo. This is particularly important if the representative does not have the authority to commit resources for their organization.

Keep a record of all communications—it serves a purpose beyond keeping current staff informed. Use this history to bring new members up to date, especially as the alliance ages and staff or membership turns over. Assign responsibility to one person for keeping the records and passing them on when they leave.

## Keep an up-to-date work plan

In the case of most alliances—whether cooperating, coordinating, or collaborating—partners need to develop a work plan that guides and organizes their efforts as the project unfolds. While it may be a simple paragraph for a cooperative project, a work plan is a good way to let everyone know what has been accomplished and what is still to be done. Building on the decisions made for the concept paper, the work plan outlines roles and responsibilities and includes specific steps, who leads the step, and dates of completion. The work plan acts as the road map for how the work gets done and is the document that people refer to when problems or questions arise. An example of a completed, detailed work plan can be found in Appendix B on page 92.

---

**EXAMPLE**

The alliance submits a proposal (with ABC serving as the fiscal sponsor for the alliance) to the Big Bucks Foundation for a grant to cover the alliance's expenses. Big Bucks awards the grant within thirty days. The alliance then develops a detailed work plan that results in fifty representatives of young families able to influence policy makers on the proposed regulation. During the first month, the alliance recruits the families, develops the training program, identifies the site, and prepares the promotional materials. In the second month they conduct the training, and in the third month, the young families complete the advocacy work on the regulation. The alliance holds a gathering to celebrate a successful effort, thus completing the project and ending the alliance.

---

## Summary

In this chapter, we proposed a five-step process for organizations that want to make the most of their resources and provide the best service possible for their clients. The proposed process helps organizations think strategically about their assets and needs before identifying alliance outcomes and approaching potential partners. The process also offers ways to manage and implement an alliance so that it reaches its full potential. In the next chapter, we discuss some stumbling blocks for alliances and offer suggestions on how to work around these obstacles or use them to improve your current alliances.

# 3. Advancing Alliances

Alliances rarely occur without a few stumbling blocks. Such problems arise from one of two root causes—a structure that does not fit the alliance's purpose and evolution or *partner relationships* that do not work effectively. In this chapter, we address methods to advance your project beyond some of these blocks. We'll examine structural causes first.

## Alliance Structure and Evolution

In Chapters 1 and 2, we encourage leaders of nonprofits to be strategic about the type and number of alliances they form because alliances can be costly in terms of staff time, organization resources, and reputation among peers and the public. This is especially true if the alliance structure (cooperation, coordination, or collaboration) does not fit the initial purpose identified by the partners. Even if the structure was appropriate when the alliance started, alliances can become more or less complex over time, necessitating a different structure. We cover the most common structural and timing problems below and give suggestions for ameliorating the situation.

### Structure is too complex

Structure must follow function, so alliance partners must look at what they want to accomplish and develop the structure to support that work. Some groups create a collaboration agreement to implement a cooperation alliance and then find there are too many restrictions and stifling processes to follow. The alliance is not as flexible as it needs to be and the outcomes are not worth the effort involved. The first symptom alliance partners notice may be a disproportionate amount of time that the members spend focusing on process and structure rather than on implementing a project. A second symptom may be frustration over the slow pace of project development, expressed either by the leadership of one of the participating organizations or a funder. Alliance members need to admit that they have more structure, rules, and formal agreements than they need to do the job, and then set about simplifying the structure to make the project easier in terms of time and resources. The participants must be honest and flexible enough to reorganize themselves.

Here's an example. A group of refugee and immigrant organizations wants to periodically network and exchange ideas as well as explore some joint fundraising opportunities. They form a collaborative structure with a formal charter. It takes the group three meetings to hammer out the agreement, during which time some of the participants lose interest in attending the meetings and drop out. The remaining group revisits what they wanted to accomplish with the alliance and decide that they only need a loose structure and simple letter of agreement to guide their work. If all or some of the group decides to jointly pursue funding, they will structure the alliance around the work to be done and the specifics of the grant. After the stumbling start-up, the alliance gets back on track to meet the needs of the participants.

## Structure is too simple

Consider the reverse: an alliance relies solely on the techniques of cooperation when the project is really a collaboration. This may happen because some alliances spend too little time up front clarifying the elements of the memo of understanding, and quickly run into conflict. This issue is often manifested in confusion around the partners' roles and responsibilities or an inability to make timely decisions because the appropriate decision makers have not been identified. The participants have to go back and address some of the issues they have not yet agreed to in their memo of understanding. Participants may need to revisit Steps 3 and 4 in Chapter 2 to make certain they have appropriately identified the right intensity of alliance. This often leads to revising the memo of understanding.

Here's an example: Two social service organizations form an alliance to develop a joint program with the school clinics in areas where the organizations provide services. The organizations spend most of their time developing the program and very little time on clarifying their relationship, roles, and responsibilities. As a result, significant accountability issues arise, and the program's quality is not what any of the organizations want. Misunderstandings about who is managing the project at each site exacerbate the difficulties. Before they can offer a quality program, the participating organizations have to back up and clarify some of the structural issues through a formal collaboration charter.

## Partners lose interest

Successfully accomplishing some part of the alliance's purpose within the first three to six months helps keep the partners energized about the alliance. If the alliance's long-term goals will take years to accomplish, establish some interim objectives that will enable the group to feel good about themselves and allow them to communicate these successes to others in the community. Maintaining the momentum after the initial enthusiasm wears off is a challenge that most partners face sometime during the life of the alliance.

Periodically, alliances need to stop to review their progress in accomplishing initial goals. Do this informally at the end of each meeting by "taking the temperature of the group" to make sure that all problems are addressed. Or do it more formally as part of managing the process through regularly reviewing the work plan or written agreements. This review provides

It is important to keep partners energized about alliance goals.

opportunities for a "midpoint" correction in the work plan if the activities drift away from the original intent. After partners reflect on the original purpose of the alliance, they may realize it is time to celebrate the achievement of the goal and close the alliance down. Alliances that work well for the partners and accomplish the goals they set out should end when the project is complete. Sometimes partners will invite external stakeholders and the general community to celebrate the project's completion.

Developing the alliance too slowly can also cause partners to lose interest in the program or project. This is particularly tricky to identify because an alliance needs to take sufficient time at the beginning to include the right people and accurately align the structure and process with the goals. If the perception is that "nothing is happening," the alliance will wither on the vine. Individuals start to miss meetings or drop out of the partnership. One way to preempt this problem is to have some successes during the early meetings of the alliance. For example, get an article in the paper, have a joint meeting with funders, conduct a pilot effort, or survey potential customers and clients. All these events build momentum and a sense of accomplishment before the program or project is ready to launch. If the partnership seems to be losing verve, ask participants to talk about why people are not participating as fully in the process in order to understand the problem.

Here's an example. A group of five social service organizations came together to fill a community need for an information and referral system. During four meetings, they developed a loose collaboration charter. These were difficult meetings because the information and referral system they were trying to form was vague, participants were uncertain about who else should be involved, and the whole process got bogged down when more partners were recruited and the initial group work had to be repeated. By the sixth meeting, participants were frustrated—two of the original five dropped out, leaving the remaining organizational representatives to re-form as a group. Almost six months into the process the collaboration had accomplished nothing.

## Alliance fails to adapt

Alliances change over time, and the work may require a lower or higher level of intensity (and structure) than it did in its forming phase. Often the success achieved in a low-intensity alliance encourages some or all of the partners to change the project or program into a more intense alliance. The project may change from a cooperative one to a coordinative or collaborative alliance, requiring a more intense relationship than the signed agreement is capable of guiding. When this happens, it is often necessary to revisit Steps 3 and 4 identified in Chapter 2 to make the necessary adjustments to the structure and process. It is important to pay attention to this shift before negative side effects occur.

In some cases, certain members of the alliance want to move into a more complex alliance while others are content to continue the current agreement. Conflicts erupt due to incorrect assumptions and changing self-interest. When this happens, determine if the original alliance should continue and resolve the differences or end so that those interested in pursuing a new, more intense partnership may do so.

## Membership changes or fails to adapt

Over time, most alliances experience changing organizational representation. People change jobs and others are promoted into the position. Or, as the alliance changes, new partners may be included. New members may raise several problems for the alliance. Interpersonal relationships among the participants may change, in particular the informal communication that occurred with the original team. Remember that each time a new partner joins an alliance, the team needs to re-form to operate at peak levels. Go back to Steps 2 through 4 in Chapter 2 and re-form as a group. Make sure that each organization remains committed to the alliance and will continue to assign resources to it. Quickly find ways to engage the new member in team-building activities. Such activities may be a normal part of the project or a one-time action like evaluating a component or developing a plan for the future.

Decisions may slow if the new representative does not have the same level of decision-making authority in the organization as his or her predecessor. When this happens, you need to find out if this is a misperception or a real issue. If it is real, you may need to request a different representative who has more authority.

New members may not be aware of the alliance's history or of the personal commitment to the values and vision that the alliance requires. Periodically, alliances need to identify changes in their membership and what they do to make the new members part of the group. New members also need to talk about their understanding of and involvement in the alliance. Sometimes the situation calls for a planning process that starts with a look at the history of the alliance and then develops a vision for the future. An inclusive planning process will lead to greater buy-in and new life for the alliance.

Structure and relationship dynamics are often interrelated. In the following section, we look at how relationships affect the desired outcomes from the alliance.

## Relationship Dynamics

Some authors describe alliances in terms of courtship and marriage relationships.[11] This metaphor rings true on many levels because alliances are ultimately based on relationships between people. Working together in partnership involves the commitment of all partners to shared goals and to "ironing out the wrinkles" when problems arise (as they inevitably do).

**Working together in partnership involves the commitment of all partners to shared goals and to "ironing out the wrinkles" when problems arise (as they inevitably do).**

In this section, we introduce a framework based on the building blocks of good relationships—shared purpose, power, and control; a common view of interdependence; mutual trust and respect; and progress indicators for the outcomes of the project or partnership. We want to acknowledge an esteemed colleague, Chris Kloth, for sharing this framework with us. Chris's organization, ChangeWorks of the Heartland, based in Columbus, Ohio, is a consulting practice that focuses on broad-based participation strategies for long-range planning and change. Chris has used the following framework, which he calls the Working Together Benchmarks, with his clients who want to improve the effectiveness of their partnerships. The framework has six components, and each is critical in developing and maintaining a strong alliance. As the lines in the diagram (Figure 8) indicate, the components

---

[11] Rosabeth Moss Kanter, "Collaborative Advantage: The Art of Alliances," *Harvard Business Review* 72, no. 4 (July–August 1994): 6.

are linked to each other in important ways. The dotted lines illustrate where components have indirect connections and impact on each other.

The six components of the framework are

- Shared purpose
- Shared power
- Shared view of interdependence
- Mutual respect and trust
- Shared control
- Shared indicators of progress

Each of these components and their interdependence are explained further in the next section.

## Figure 8: Working Together Benchmarks

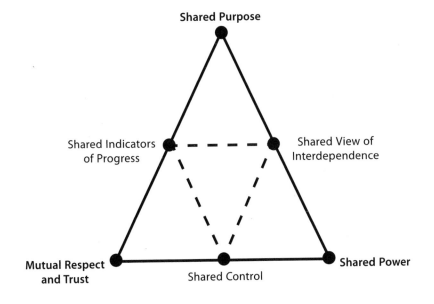

Chris Kloth developed a process using the framework components that helps alliance partners surface underlying issues impeding their progress. Deceptively simple but effective, the process uses facilitated conversations on the six factors to help partners to identify which approaches to working together are the most appropriate for their alliance. As you become aware of concerns you and your partners have about your alliance or the results it is achieving, we suggest that you use the following questions as a guide for your discussions.

1. *Shared purpose:* Do we (each organization) have the same goals for the alliance? Develop a detailed, qualitative, and descriptive understanding of what the alliance should be achieving.

2. *Shared power:* What knowledge, skills, relationships, and staff do we need to accomplish the purpose of this alliance?

3. *Shared view of interdependence:* Do we really believe that we are interdependent? Why do we need each other to accomplish the goal the way we aspire to?

4. *Mutual respect and trust:* Did each of us do what we agreed to do?

5. *Shared control:* Are we sharing resources in a complete and timely way?

6. *Shared indicators of progress:* In areas where we are progressing toward our shared purpose, what can we do to improve our results? Where we aren't progressing toward our shared purpose, what is making it hard to move forward?

Ask an outside facilitator to help with this conversation. A skilled, neutral facilitator can structure the conversation so that all partners will have equal voice, stay on task, and conclude with action steps.

The next sections give more background about the importance of each component to the overall success of the alliance.

## Shared purpose

As mentioned in Chapter 1, alliances must be based on shared goals and create win-win outcomes for all partners. Over time these goals may be almost completed or may change due to the changing needs of clients or the community. To keep the momentum of the alliance going or ensure that its purpose is still on target, partners should periodically have a conversation to review their shared purpose. Begin the process with the question, *Do we have the same goals for the alliance?* Be sure that the conversation results in a detailed description of the alliance's intended outcomes in concrete terms or relevant metrics. Partners often agree to a general idea, but when they get to specifics they find that each organization had in mind different outcomes or assumed a different use of resources.

For example, an alliance between a neighborhood elementary school and a large hospital has a purpose of providing an "in-house" clinic at the school. At first, the partners described their purpose as establishing a small clinic somewhere in the school. It was more helpful for the alliance to be specific, beginning with the following:

> The clinic, painted in bright primary colors, is located in the east wing of the school. As they walk in the door, a nurse greets our young patients and leads them directly to a room. An entrance ramp into the building makes the clinic easily accessible from both the school and the street. Doctors and nurses from the local hospital staff the clinic from 8 a.m. to 3 p.m. Monday through Friday . . .

This discussion often gives partners a clearer idea of what they want to accomplish and can help them identify and claim aspects like organizational values, governance policies, or employment contracts that are nonnegotiable in the context of this alliance. In the example above, it is possible that the doctors can only staff the clinic from 10 a.m. to 2 p.m. Monday through Wednesday. This is an important detail for the alliance to plan around.

Once alliance partners clarify and agree on their shared purpose, they are ready to move to a discussion on their shared power.

### Shared power

The primary reason that organizations form alliances is that they lack resources needed to accomplish an important goal, and partners bring those resources into the alliance. In an effective alliance, the partners need each other and recognize the contributions each brings to the alliance. These contributions are usually not the same, but they are equally necessary for success. For example, one partner may bring financial support, another connections to the target clients, and another meeting or program space in their facility. Sometimes the organization that provides the financial support is perceived as providing the most valued resource and therefore, as having the greater power or decision-making authority. Clearly state the equal value of each of the partner's contributions early in the alliance and be vigilant that power differentials don't develop over time among partners.

If one organization feels undervalued, its commitment to the alliance or to its willingness to provide the necessary resources may be affected. Building on their description of the alliance's purpose, partners will ask, *What knowledge, skills, relationships, and staff (or other resources) are necessary to accomplish the purpose?* In the example of the school clinic alliance, the resources needed were, among many others, the skills of doctors and nurses and the location inside a school. If the outcomes of the project are not emerging as expected, partners should review who has agreed to be responsible for and has the power to accomplish what portion of the outcomes.

### Shared view of interdependence

Partners of successful alliances recognize that they depend on each other for achieving the goals of the alliance. After talking about their shared purpose and power, partners need to conduct a reality check. Engage partners in a conversation on the questions, *Do we really believe that we are interdependent? Why do we need each other to accomplish the purpose to which we aspire?* These questions will help partners understand where they are interdependent and where they are independent. If one or more of the partners thinks they could have the same impact on their own or that others in the alliance won't follow through on their commitments, the partners should seriously reevaluate continuing their alliance. In the example of the school clinic, the hospital needs a location that is convenient for its patients, and the school can't afford the expense of providing its own nursing services. Their dependence on one another is based on the elements of this framework—a shared sense of purpose, power, control, and indicators of progress. Mutual trust and respect make organizations willing to depend on each other in this manner. If partners begin to act independently—breaking agreements, skipping meetings, or not following though with promised resources—take a look at each organization's view of interdependence, mutual respect, and trust among partners.

## Mutual respect and trust

Many alliances begin with a positive personal relationship between two top executives and the enthusiasm of seeing a great idea come together. Once the alliance moves from the "great idea" stage to the implementation stage, the relationships between people who are actually doing the work become critical. Mutual respect and trust need to be nurtured among alliance representatives at all levels of the project. If these qualities are missing, the alliance may never achieve its full potential. Therefore, organizations should include a team-building component in their alliance planning efforts so that positive relationships begin to form immediately and are maintained over time. Organizations that work together for an extended period of time or on several successful projects sometimes find they are comfortable giving up more control on decision making because they have built up trust in their partners.

> Organizations should include a team-building component in their alliance planning efforts so that positive relationships begin to form immediately and are maintained over time.

Many successful alliances begin with small, short-term projects that help to build trust between organizations. Leaders gradually build on these initial successes as more long-term, intensive relationships develop. As Karen Ray points out in *The Nimble Collaboration,* "Trust is a key indicator of the potential for success. Trust happens as you work. Build trust by sharing data and clarifying expectations."[12] Ray's definition of trust in a partnership is

---

[12]  Ray, *The Nimble Collaboration,* 33.

shared hope and a personal energy for honesty. To better understand if mutual respect and trust are still strong or have diminished over time, partners will ask, *Do we believe we can accomplish our goals? Did each of us do what we said we would do?* The answer to these questions often leads partners to talk about what has been and what needs to be accomplished.

### Shared control

The link between shared power and mutual respect and trust is shared control. Control in this context is the system or systems alliance partners put in place to ensure that shared resources are used effectively and efficiently. The work plan partners develop as they begin an alliance is an example of a system that spells out what activities will happen, when they will happen, and who will be responsible for ensuring that they happen. Other systems might be blueprints and building specs, contracts, or policies and procedures. The project dictates the form of the control, but all systems need to be as transparent as possible to allow the partners to provide and receive timely feedback and make adjustments if necessary. Building on the conversation about shared purpose, power, and view of interdependence, partners will ask, *Are we sharing the resources needed for the alliance in a complete and timely way?* In the example of the school clinic, contracts stipulate specific deliverables—the hospital ensures that adequate health care staff is present when the clinic is open, and the school ensures that the offices are well maintained and comfortable. Regular appraisal of what has been accomplished and shared indicators of progress keep alliances healthy.

### Shared indicators of progress

To sustain an alliance over time, partners must feel that they are successfully accomplishing goals. While this is difficult to do, it is also critical if the alliance is to stay together. If the alliance is using Kloth's framework to structure a discussion, partners will conclude with the questions, *In areas where we are progressing toward our shared purpose, what can we do to improve our results? Where we aren't progressing toward our shared purpose, what is making it hard to move forward?* By this time in the discussion, the partners should have a better understanding of how their alliance operates and may have some ideas for making it even better. The key to this conversation is focusing on what difference the alliance makes in the lives of its clients or in its community rather than on judging each partner's performance. This is often a time to collect and examine specific numbers or measurements. In the spirit of shared power, control, and mutual respect and trust, deliver the results in a way that enhances the quality of the work and the working relationships. In the school clinic example, school and hospital partners find that parents are not aware of the clinic's many services and tend to use it less than the alliance had anticipated. Partners then decide to heavily market the clinic for a month through flyers in school bags and posters at the hospital to increase the numbers of children served. Identifying and agreeing on indicators of progress can give an alliance new energy and allow the purpose to evolve with the needs of the community it serves.

One of the greatest benefits in following the Working Together Benchmarks is the strengthening of relationships among alliance partners as they take time to talk with each other and focus on the purpose for their alliance. If your alliance is searching for a complementary resource, we recommend "The Wilder Collaboration Factors Inventory." It is an excellent tool for evaluating and analyzing how an alliance is operating. While the inventory is designed particularly for collaborations, all types of alliances can benefit from paying attention to the factors and how they work together. The inventory, along with in-depth guidance on interpreting it, is in the book, *Collaboration: What Makes It Work* [13] or order it online at www.FieldstoneAlliance.org.

[13]   Mattessich, *Collaboration: What Makes It Work,* 37.

# Conclusion

During the late 1980s and 90s funders, government officials, and non-profit leaders looked at forming alliances as the response to increasing demand and scarce resources. In some instances, establishing collaborations became an end in itself with mixed results. We would like to see the idea of forming alliances considered strategically and neither embraced too quickly nor dismissed out of hand. Since "one size" does not fit all, we believe that different leaders, organizations, and issues should make use of the different forms of alliances.

In this book, we have tried to give people a new perspective on forming alliances by fleshing out the different levels of working together and demonstrating when and how to use each. We had three goals in this process:

- Propose the alliance continuum as a valuable way to look at different ways to work together.
- Make a case for forming alliances at the lowest levels of intensity because they
  - May make most sense given the problem or opportunity
  - Offer low risk opportunities to try working with others to see if future collaboration might make sense
  - Allow organizations to connect with many more organizations on a regular basis
- Provide a process, structure, and tools for exploring, forming, and maintaining alliances.

We hope that in this book we have broadened the discussion on forming alliances, piqued leaders interest in looking at all the partnering options, and provided the reader with additional tools for the toolkit that nonprofits use to strengthen our communities.

Appendix A

# Worksheets

The following worksheets can be downloaded at the publisher's web site at the following URL. Simply enter this URL in your web browser and use the following code to download the materials. If you have any difficulties, phone the publisher at 800-274-6024.

http://www.FieldstoneAlliance.org/worksheets

Code: W466FFa05

These materials are intended for use in the same way as photocopies, but they are in a form that allows you to type in your responses and reformat the worksheets. Please do not download the material unless you or your organization has purchased this book.

## Worksheet 1   Clarify the Purpose of the Alliance

*Use this worksheet as a guide to help you think strategically about a possible alliance.*

### Instructions

❑  Complete as much as possible as you begin the discussion within your own organization.

❑  After each planning meeting, revise and add to this worksheet based on the leadership team's input.

### Service delivery

1.  Do we have some desired outcomes that we have not been able to achieve on our own?

2.  Are there some strategies that we would like to implement but need more resources to do so? What kind of resources?

### External environment

3.  Is system advocacy important for accomplishing our mission?

4. Do we want to change the way the service system operates? If so, how?

**Internal capacity**

5. What are the key values in our organization?

6. What will we not compromise on?

7. Are there some administrative services that we need but cannot afford?

## Worksheet 2  Develop the Concept Paper

*Use this worksheet as a guide to help you develop a concept paper for your alliance.*

### Instructions

- ❏ Complete as much as possible prior to your first planning meeting, noting that it is a draft.

- ❏ Refer to the sample concept paper in Appendix B to see how each section could be written.

- ❏ After each planning meeting, revise and add to this document based on the group's input.

- ❏ When the draft is final, format it into a document that can be used for potential funders or sponsors.

### History

1. What work will the alliance build on? Who else has been involved in addressing the issue?

### Outcomes

2. Why do you want to start an alliance? What do you want the alliance to accomplish? What conditions make the alliance goals timely or urgent?

**Scale or scope**

3.  How quickly are outcomes needed? What is the time frame? How many partners need to be involved? How many clients does the alliance hope to impact? What kinds of resources or skills are required for maximum effectiveness?

**First steps**

4.  Who is most likely to be interested or want to be involved? What are their resources and skills?

## Worksheet 3  What Do We Have to Offer a Partner?

*Use this worksheet as a guide to help you identify and recruit partners to participate in the alliance.*

### Instructions
❏  Your organization's leadership should discuss the following questions.

### Service delivery
1.  Do we have unique services or programs?

### Internal capacity
2.  Do we have an exceptional infrastructure, such as an accurate record-keeping and reporting system or an extraordinary marketing department?

3.  Do we have other resources we can share with others (for example, an excellent mailing list or a host of volunteers)?

4.  Do we have experience working in alliances?

**External environment**

5.  Do we have a solid reputation in the community and with funders?

6.  Do we have special access to different sectors of our community?

## Worksheet 4  Identify and Recruit Partners

*Use this worksheet as a guide to help you identify and recruit partners to participate in the alliance.*

### Instructions

❑ Ask leadership in the organization to brainstorm a list of organizations based on the questions below.

❑ After developing a list, compare it with the goals set forth in the concept paper to determine whether these people would be interested in participating in an alliance.

❑ Once the list has been affirmed, identify someone to approach each potential partner. (This will usually be someone who has a personal or professional relationship with the decision maker.)

1. Who are the leaders in our field of work?

2. With whom have we worked before?

3. Who are our competitors?

4. With whom should we work for either informational reasons or political reasons or both?

5. Who has the skills, technical capabilities, or assets that we need and don't have?

| Potential Partner | Who Will Contact | By When | Notes |
|---|---|---|---|
| | | | |
| | | | |
| | | | |
| | | | |
| | | | |
| | | | |
| | | | |
| | | | |
| | | | |
| | | | |
| | | | |
| | | | |

## Worksheet 5   Frame the Alliance

*Use this worksheet to help decide whether to proceed with any form of alliance.*

### Instructions

❑   At an initial meeting of potential partners, discuss the questions below to disclose self-interests, decide what form of alliance is necessary, and determine what resources are needed. At this meeting, some participants may decide that they cannot participate. Others will state an intent to proceed.

❑   After the meeting, revise the concept paper with the group's decisions and decide whether to recruit additional partners in order to proceed.

❑   When the concept paper draft is final, format it into a document that can be used for potential funders or sponsors.

1.  What does each organization find interesting about this concept? How does it fit with the organization's mission? What needs would it address in the organization and in the community?

2.  Who else might be interested in the concept?

3. What roles and responsibilities make sense given the skills of the people involved and the size and scope of the alliance project?

4. Given the goals agreed to in the concept paper, at what level do we want to frame the alliance (cooperation, coordination, or collaboration)?

5. What are our next steps?

## Worksheet 6   Formalize the Structure and Plan for Success

*Use this worksheet as a guide to help you develop a plan, structure, and budget for the alliance.*

### Instructions

❑ As you begin to meet with your partners, use this worksheet to record your discussion. Note: The discussion may not be linear but skip around the topics as people talk about what is most important to them. This worksheet gives you a way to ensure that all the major ones are covered.

**Strategic Alliance Title:** _____

**Mission/Purpose Statement:** (What good, for whom?)

Hint: Don't forget about geography if it is defining.

**Two to Three Key Outcomes:** (What will be different in future?)

Hint: Try to frame this for customers or clients.

**Strategies:** (How will the outcomes be achieved?)

Hint: This is where you will begin to broadly describe the program/project.

**Known Resources:** (What resources do you need?)

Hint: Don't forget about skills, knowledge, access.

**Potential Partners:** (Who should be at the table?)

Hint: Remember self-interest is important for partners.

**Stakeholders:** (Who has an interest in what you will do?)

Hint: Think about people's perceptions.

**Time frame:** (When will the project/program start?)

Hint: Remember to plan for fundraising and promotion.

**Decision making:** (How will decisions be made and who needs to be involved?)

**Communication:** (How will we keep internal stakeholders engaged and informed? Who is responsible for communicating with external stakeholders?)

**Showstoppers:** (What might keep the program/project from happening?)

Hint: Think beyond fundraising.

# Examples

## Sample Concept Paper

ABC Project Concept Paper:

# How to involve young parents in advocating for proposed school regulation

### Background of this idea

ABC's mission is to advocate for the rights of people with disabilities. In the past few years, we have been concerned about how to best advocate for young parents with children who have disabilities—especially since a recently proposed school regulation will have a huge impact on their lives. To sufficiently influence policy makers, these parents need to be educated on the issues and involved in advocating for the new regulation. Their involvement will give ABC's advocacy work the necessary visible support of young families. However, few young parents participate in ABC's advocacy programs, preferring to join XYZ for their relevant information and support groups or LMN for their help in addressing problems in the school system. ABC recognizes that young parents have a limited amount of free time and wants to make it easy for them to participate in its advocacy efforts. In addition, ABC needs to be a good steward of its resources and not compete for clients with other organizations that are providing excellent complementary services.

### Purpose of the alliance

The purpose of this alliance is to

- Share information about the proposed school regulation
- Recruit young parents into the project
- Provide training to young parents so that they can assist in revising the proposed school regulation
- Defray the costs of parent involvement in the project

### Outcomes

An alliance of ABC, XYZ, and LMN (and perhaps other partners) will directly impact people with disabilities and their families and make a difference in their lives for years to come. The involvement of informed, concerned constituents will influence policy makers and help to make needed revisions in the proposed school regulation.

**The first steps**

Before the end of the summer, we will need to

1. Assign a lead organization to manage the advocacy component

2. Recruit young parents of disabled children who are willing to advocate for revising the proposed school regulation

3. Provide a comprehensive training program for the young parents so they understand the roles of each of the participating organizations, the background on the proposed regulation and the regulation's probable impact on students

4. Involve the informed young parents in meetings the State Department of Education will hold on the regulation

This project will be complete by the end of December when the vote will be taken on the school regulation. At that time, we could decide to continue as an alliance to advocate for other issues or celebrate our success and conclude the alliance project.

## Sample Memo of Understanding

Memo of Understanding for

- Nonprofit Capacity Builders, Inc.
- The Community College of Business Practices
- The Local Management Training Institute
- Youth Links to Excellence
- Northern Advocacy and Policy Center

This serves as a memo of understanding among our five organizations approved on (date)_____. Our purpose for this cooperative effort is to share information and materials with each other to avoid duplication of effort and to support each other's work through referrals. We may also co-sponsor events or activities when the timing, resources, and community needs are advantageous. We will write a separate agreement among participating partners in that event.

We will hold monthly meetings on the second Monday of each month from noon to 2:00 p.m. The agenda for each meeting will include time to share information about our work, highlight new programming, conferences, and workshops, and expand our collegial working relationships.

The meeting will be hosted by members in rotation. The host's responsibilities are to:

- Select the location of the meeting
- Arrange for all logistics such as room arrangement and meeting setup
- Send out a meeting reminder to all members with meeting location and directions

Member's responsibilities are

- To attend meetings prepared to participate
- Bring copies of handouts for all members
- Act as host every 5 months
- Bring their own brown bag lunch or some food to share

We will revisit this memo of understanding annually at our December meeting.

## Sample Letter of Agreement

## Parent Involvement Alliance Letter of Agreement

The Young Parents Involvement Project is a voluntary alliance among the following organizations:

- ABC
- LMN
- Legal Aid to Parents
- XYZ

These organizations all serve people with disabilities and their families. The purposes of this project are to

1. Recruit more young parents of disabled children from the programming of LMN and XYZ to actively advocate for the proposed school regulation.

2. Provide a comprehensive training program for young parents so they understand the roles of each of the participating organizations, the background on the proposed regulation, and the regulation's probable impact on students.

3. Involve the informed young parents in meetings the State Department of Education will hold on the regulation.

The alliance commits to

- Sharing information about the new school regulation
- Recruiting young parents into the project
- Providing training to young parents, so they can assist in revising the proposed school regulation
- Defraying the costs of parent involvement in the project

ABC will serve as the fiscal sponsor for the project and will take the lead in managing the advocacy component of the project.

LMN and XYZ will recruit young parents to participate in the project.

Legal Aid to Parents will provide training to help parents understand the issues involved in the proposed school regulation and enable them to effectively participate in the review and comment process.

A budget of $5,000 is needed to implement the program as follows:

| Item | Amount | Use |
|---|---|---|
| Recruitment brochures | $ 2,000 | Recruiting young parents |
| Meeting room | 500 | Training space |
| Travel expenses | 1,000 | Travel costs of parents and professionals |
| Child care | 1,500 | Care for children of parents during participation |
| **Total** | **$ 5,000** | |

The alliance will strive to make all decisions by consensus; however, the fiscal sponsor is responsible for seeing that the grant is spent in accordance with the budget. We agree that the executive directors will represent their organizations and make every effort to attend every meeting. In the rare case that a director will be absent, the organization may appoint one alternate with voting rights.

Our organizations and the following representatives commit to participation in this project.


Authorized Signature: _____Date: _____

Printed Name: _____Title: _____

Organization: _____


Authorized Signature: _____Date: _____

Printed Name: _____Title: _____

Organization: _____

Authorized Signature: _____Date: _____

Printed Name: _____Title: _____

Organization: _____


Authorized Signature: _____Date: _____

Printed Name: _____Title: _____

Organization: _____

## Sample Work Plan

Parent Involvement Alliance (ABC, LMN, Legal Aid to Parents, XYZ

Project Management Work Plan

| Strategies and Action Steps | Lead Organization | By When |
|---|---|---|
| 1. Develop a work plan to manage the project | ABC | July |
| 2. Recruit young parents who are willing to advocate for revising the proposed school regulation<br>a. Distribute information sheets on the regulation and alliance formation at all meetings with clients<br>b. At each support group, hold an information session on alliance goals<br>c. Schedule phone conversations with people who indicate an interest in participating | XYZ, LMN | Aug |
| 3. Provide a comprehensive training program for the young parents that includes<br>a. Information on the alliance's purpose<br>b. Background on the regulation<br>c. The regulation's probable impact on students | ABC, Legal Aid to Parents | Sept |
| 4. Involve the informed young parents in meetings the State Department of Education will hold on the regulation<br>a. Find out scheduled meeting dates<br>b. Get parents signed up for the meetings<br>c. Provide parents with "talking points" | ABC | Oct |
| 5. Schedule follow-up meetings between individual policy makers and young parents | ABC, Parents | Nov |

# Bibliography

## Books

Angelica, Emil. *Crafting Effective Mission & Vision Statements*. Saint Paul, MN: Fieldstone Alliance, 2001.

Angelica, Emil, and Vincent Hyman. *Coping with Cutbacks: The Nonprofit Guide to Success When Times Are Tight*. Saint Paul, MN: Fieldstone Alliance, 1997.

Arsenault, Jane. *Forging Nonprofit Alliances*. San Francisco, CA: Jossey-Bass, 1996.

Bartling, Charles. *Strategic Alliances for Nonprofit Organizations*. Washington, DC: American Society of Association Executives, 1998.

Connolly, Paul, and Carol Lukas. *Strengthening Nonprofit Performance: A Funder's Guide to Capacity Building*. Saint Paul, MN: Fieldstone Alliance, 2002.

Doz, Yves, and Gary Hamel. *Alliance Advantage: The Art of Creating Value through Partnering*. Boston, MA: Harvard Business School Press, 1998.

Harbison, John, and Peter Pekar Jr. Smart *Alliances: A Practical Guide to Repeatable Success*. San Francisco, CA: Booz-Allen & Hamilton Inc., 1998.

LaPiana, David. *The Nonprofit Mergers Workbook*. Saint Paul, MN: Fieldstone Alliance, 2000.

Lukas, Carol, and Linda Hoskins. *Conducting Community Forums: Engaging Citizens, Mobilizing Communities*. Saint Paul, MN: Fieldstone Alliance, 2002.

Mattessich, Paul W., Marta Murray-Close, and Barbara Monsey. *Collaboration: What Makes It Work. 2nd ed.* Saint Paul, MN: Fieldstone Alliance, 2001.

McLaughlin, Thomas. *Nonprofit Mergers and Alliances: A Strategic Planning Guide.* New York: John Wiley & Sons, 1998.

Ray, Karen. *The Nimble Collaboration: Fine-Tuning Your Collaboration for Lasting Success.* Saint Paul, MN: Fieldstone Alliance, 2002.

Sandler, Martin, and Deborah Hudson. *Beyond the Bottom Line: How to Do More with Less in Nonprofit and Public Organizations.* Cary, NC: Oxford University Press, 2001.

Winer, Michael, and Karen Ray. *Collaboration Handbook: Creating, Sustaining, and Enjoying the Journey.* Saint Paul, MN: Fieldstone Alliance, 1994.

## Periodicals

Alter, Catherine, and Jerald Hage. *Organizations Working Together.* Newbury Park, CA: Sage Library of Social Research, 1993.

Babbio, Lawrence T., Jr. "Alliances, Partnerships: Making the Marriage Work." *America's Network 100*, no. 13 (July 1, 1996): 22.

Baum, Geoff, et al. "Introducing the New Value Creation Index." *Forbes ASAP* (April 3, 2000). <http://www.forbes.com/asap/2000/0403/140.html>

Douma, Marc, Jan Bilderbeek, Peter Idenburg, and Jan Kees Looise. "Strategic Alliances: Managing the Dynamics of Fit." *Long Range Planning* 33, no. 4 (August 2000): 579–98.

Dyer, Jeffrey, Prashant Kale, and Harbir Singh. "How to Make Strategic Alliances Work." *MIT Sloan Management Review* 42 (Summer 2001): 37–43.

Gais, Thomas, Courtney Burke, and Rebecca Corso. "A Divided Community: The Effects of State Fiscal Crises on Nonprofits Providing Health and Social Assistance," a working paper from the Aspen Institute's Nonprofit Sector Research Fund (2003): xx.

Gonzalez, Maria. "Strategic Alliances." *Ivey Business Journal* 66, no. 1 (September–October 2001): 47–51.

James, Katherine. "Understanding Successful Partnerships and Collaborations." *P & R* (May 1999): 39–47.

Kalmbach, Charles, Jr. and Charles Roussel. "Dispelling the Myths of Alliances." *Outlook Online* (Accenture Consulting: October 1999). <http://www.accenture.com/xd/xd.asp?it=enweb&xd=ideas\outlook\special99\over_specialed_intro.xml>

Kanter, Rosabeth Moss. "Collaborative Advantage: The Art of Alliances." *Harvard Business Review* 72, no. 4 (July–August 1994): 96–108.

Kuglin, Fred A. "New Realities of Alliance Partnering." *Financial Executive* 18, no. 9 (December 2002): 30–34.

La Piana, David. "Real Collaboration: A Guide for Grantmakers." A report written at the request of the Ford Foundation (January 2001). <http://www.lapiana.org/research/real.html>

Lesky, Steven, Elizabethann O'Sullivan, and Barbara Goodmon. "Local Public-Nonprofit Partnerships: Getting Better Results." *Policy & Practice of Public Human Services* 59, no. 3 (September 2001): 28.

Mason, Julie. "Strategic Alliances: Partnering for Success." *Management Review* 82 (May 1993): 10.

Meyer, Lisa. "Working in Tandem: The Art of Partnering—Five steps to a Fruitful Relationship." *VAR Business* (December 16, 2002): 54.

Morrison, Michael, and Larissa Mezentseff. "Learning Alliances: A New Dimension of Strategic Alliances." *Management Decision* 35, no. 5 (1977): 351–57.

Parise, Salvatore, and Lisa Sasson. "Leveraging Knowledge Management Across Strategic Alliances." *Ivey Business Journal* 66, no. 4 (March–April 2002): 41–47.

Rackham, Neil. "The Pitfalls of Partnering: Follow These Three Steps to Determine Whether You Should Find a Partner Or Fly Solo." *Sales & Marketing Management* (April 2001): 32–33.

Rapp, Canon Phillip J. "For-profit and Not-for-profit Alliances: Possibilities and Realities." *Behavioral Health Management* 18, no. 2 (March 1998): 31–33.

Rondinelli, Dennis, and Ted London. "Nonprofit-Corporate Alliances: Risks, Opportunities, and Guidelines." *Snapshots* (November 2001)<http://www.nonprofitresearch.org/usr_doc/01-N%20(SNAPSHOTS).pdf>

Rule, Erik, and Nicholas Ross. "Beating the Odds: Making a Strategic Alliance Succeed." *Pharmaceutical Executive* 19 (January 1999): 78–83.

Salamon, Lester M., and Richard O'Sullivan. "Stressed but Coping: Nonprofit Organizations and the Current Fiscal Crisis," *Communiqué #2* from the Listening Post Project, Johns Hopkins University Institute for Policy Studies, Center for Civil Society Studies (January 19, 2004): 4. <http://www.jhu.edu/listeningpost/news/pdf/comm02.pdf>

Segil, Larraine. "Understanding Life Cycle Differences." *Association Management* 52, no. 8 (2000): 32–33.

Takahashi, Lois M., and Gayla Smutny. "Collaborative Windows and Organizational Governance: Exploring the Formation and Demise of Social Service Partnerships." *Nonprofit and Voluntary Sector Quarterly* 31, no. 2 (June 2002): 165–85.

Vangen, Siv, and Chris Huxham. "Nurturing Collaborative Relations: Building Trust in Interorganizational Collaboration." *The Journal of Applied Behavioral Science* 39, no. 1 (March 2003): 5.

Yankey, John A., Amy McClellan, and Barbara Wester Jacobus. *Nonprofit Strategic Alliances Case Studies: Lessons from the Trenches.* Cleveland, OH: Mandel Center for Nonprofit Organizations, Case Western Reserve University, 2001.

# More results-oriented books from Fieldstone Alliance

## Collaboration

### Collaboration Handbook
Creating, Sustaining, and Enjoying the Journey
*by Michael Winer and Karen Ray*

Shows you how to get a collaboration going, set goals, determine everyone's roles, create an action plan, and evaluate the results. Includes a case study of one collaboration from start to finish, helpful tips on how to avoid pitfalls, and worksheets to keep everyone on track.

*192 pages, softcover     Item # 069032*

### Collaboration: What Makes It Work, 2nd Ed.
*by Paul Mattessich, PhD, Marta Murray-Close, BA, and Barbara Monsey, MPH*

An in-depth review of current collaboration research. Major findings are summarized, critical conclusions are drawn, and twenty key factors influencing successful collaborations are identified. Includes The Wilder Collaboration Factors Inventory, which groups can use to assess their collaboration.

*104 pages, softcover     Item # 069326*

A Fieldstone Nonprofit Guide to
### Forming Alliances
*by Linda Hoskins and Emil Angelica*

Helps you understand the wide range of ways that they can work with others—focusing on alliances that work at a lower level of intensity. It shows how to plan and start an alliance that fits a nonprofit's circumstances and needs.

*112 pages, softcover     Item # 069466*

### The Nimble Collaboration
Fine-Tuning Your Collaboration for Lasting Success
*by Karen Ray*

Shows you ways to make your existing collaboration more responsive, flexible, and productive. Provides three key strategies to help your collaboration respond quickly to changing environments and participants.

*136 pages, softcover     Item # 069288*

## Management & Planning

### Benchmarking for Nonprofits
How to Measure, Manage, and Improve Performance
*by Jason Saul*

Benchmarking—the onging process of measuring your organization against leaders—can help stimulate innovation, increase your impact, decrease your costs, raise money, inspire your staff, impress your funders, engage your board, and sharpen your mission. This book defines a formal, systematic, and reliable way to benchmark, from preparing your organization to measuring performance and implementing best practices.

*112 pages, softcover     Item # 069431*

### The Best of the Board Café
Hands-on Solutions for Nonprofit Boards
*by Jan Masaoka, CompassPoint Nonprofit Services*

Gathers the most requested articles from the e-newsletter, *Board Café*. You'll find a lively menu of ideas, information, opinions, news, and resources to help board members give and get the most out of their board service.

*232 pages, softcover     Item # 069407*

### Consulting with Nonprofits: A Practitioner's Guide
*by Carol A. Lukas*

A step-by-step, comprehensive guide for consultants. Addresses the art of consulting, how to run your business, and much more. Also includes tips and anecdotes from thirty skilled consultants.

*240 pages, softcover     Item # 069172*

The Fieldstone Nonprofit Guide to
### Crafting Effective Mission and Vision Statements
*by Emil Angelica*

Guides you through two six-step processes that result in a mission statement, vision statement, or both. Shows how a clarified mission and vision lead to more effective leadership, decisions, fundraising, and management. Includes tips, sample statements, and worksheets.

*88 pages, softcover     Item # 06927X*

**For current prices, a catalog, or to order call 800-274-6024**

The Fieldstone Nonprofit Guide to
## Developing Effective Teams
*by Beth Gilbertsen and Vijit Ramchandani*

Helps you understand, start, and maintain a team. Provides tools and techniques for writing a mission statement, setting goals, conducting effective meetings, creating ground rules to manage team dynamics, making decisions in teams, creating project plans, and developing team spirit.

*80 pages, softcover        Item # 069202*

## The Five Life Stages of Nonprofit Organizations
Where You Are, Where You're Going, and What to Expect When You Get There
*by Judith Sharken Simon with J. Terence Donovan*

Shows you what's "normal" for each development stage which helps you plan for transitions, stay on track, and avoid unnecessary struggles. Includes The Nonprofit Life Stage Assessment to plot your organization's progress in seven arenas of organization development.

*128 pages, softcover        Item # 069229*

## The Lobbying and Advocacy Handbook for Nonprofit Organizations
Shaping Public Policy at the State and Local Level
*by Marcia Avner*

*The Lobbying and Advocacy Handbook* is a planning guide and resource for nonprofit organizations that want to influence issues that matter to them. This book will help you decide whether to lobby and then put plans in place to make it work.

*240 pages, softcover        Item # 069261*

## The Manager's Guide to Program Evaluation:
Planning, Contracting, and Managing for Useful Results
*by Paul W. Mattessich, Ph.D.*

Explains how to plan and manage an evaluation that will help identify your organization's successes, share information with key audiences, and improve services.

*96 pages, softcover        Item # 069385*

## The Nonprofit Board Member's Guide to Lobbying and Advocacy
*by Marcia Avner*

Written specifically for board members, this guide helps organizations increase their impact on policy decisions. It reveals how board members can be involved in planning for and implementing successful lobbying efforts.

*96 pages, softcover        Item # 069393*

## The Nonprofit Mergers Workbook
The Leader's Guide to Considering, Negotiating, and Executing a Merger
*by David La Piana*

A merger can be a daunting and complex process. Save time, money, and untold frustration with this highly practical guide that makes the process manageable and controllable. Includes case studies, decision trees, twenty-two worksheets, checklists, tips, and complete step-by-step guidance from seeking partners to writing the merger agreement, and more.

*240 pages, softcover        Item # 069210*

## The Nonprofit Mergers Workbook Part II
Unifying the Organization after a Merger
*by La Piana Associates*

Once the merger agreement is signed, the question becomes: How do we make this merger work? *Part II* helps you create a comprehensive plan to achieve *integration*—bringing together people, programs, processes, and systems from two (or more) organizations into a single, unified whole.

*248 pages, includes CD-ROM   Item # 069415*

## Nonprofit Stewardship
A Better Way to Lead Your Mission-Based Organization
*by Peter C. Brinckerhoff*

The stewardship model of leadership can help your organization improve its mission capability by forcing you to keep your organization's mission foremost. It helps you make decisions that are best for the people your organization serves. In other words, stewardship helps you do more good for more people.

*272 pages, softcover        Item # 069423*

## Resolving Conflict in Nonprofit Organizations
The Leader's Guide to Finding Constructive Solutions
*by Marion Peters Angelica*

Helps you identify conflict, decide whether to intervene, uncover and deal with the true issues, and design and conduct a conflict resolution process. Includes exercises to learn and practice conflict resolution skills, guidance on handling unique conflicts such as harassment and discrimination, and when (and where) to seek outside help with litigation, arbitration, and mediation.

*192 pages, softcover        Item # 069164*

**For current prices visit us online at 🖥 www.FieldstoneAlliance.org**

## Strategic Planning Workbook for Nonprofit Organizations, Revised and Updated
*by Bryan Barry*

Chart a wise course for your nonprofit's future. This time-tested workbook gives you practical step-by-step guidance, real-life examples, one nonprofit's complete strategic plan, and easy-to-use worksheets.

*144 pages, softcover      Item # 069075*

## Finances

### Bookkeeping Basics
What Every Nonprofit Bookkeeper Needs to Know
*by Debra L. Ruegg and Lisa M. Venkatrathnam*

This book will enable you to successfully meet the basic bookkeeping requirements of your nonprofit organization—even if you have no formal accounting training.

*128 pages, softcover      Item # 069296*

### Coping with Cutbacks:
The Nonprofit Guide to Success When Times Are Tight
*by Emil Angelica and Vincent Hyman*

Shows you practical ways to involve business, government, and other nonprofits to solve problems together. Also includes 185 cutback strategies you can put to use right away.

*128 pages, softcover      Item # 069091*

### Financial Leadership for Nonprofit Executives
Guiding Your Organization to Long-term Success
*Jeanne Bell Peters and Elizabeth Schaffer*

Provides executives with a practical guide to protecting and growing the assets of their organizations and with accomplishing as much mission as possible with those resources.

*144 pages, softcover      Item # 06944X*

### Venture Forth! The Essential Guide to Starting a Moneymaking Business in Your Nonprofit Organization
*by Rolfe Larson*

The most complete guide on nonprofit business development. Building on the experience of dozens of organizations, this handbook gives you a time-tested approach for finding, testing, and launching a successful nonprofit business venture.

*272 pages, softcover      Item # 069245*

## Marketing & Fundraising

The Fieldstone Nonprofit Guide to
### Conducting Successful Focus Groups
*by Judith Sharken Simon*

Shows how to collect valuable information without a lot of money or special expertise. Using this proven technique, you'll get essential opinions and feedback to help you check out your assumptions, do better strategic planning, improve services or products, and more.

*80 pages, softcover      Item # 069199*

### Marketing Workbook for Nonprofit Organizations Volume I: Develop the Plan
*by Gary J. Stern*

Don't just wish for results—get them! Here's how to create a straightforward, usable marketing plan. Includes the six Ps of Marketing, how to use them effectively, a sample marketing plan, tips on using the Internet, and worksheets.

*208 pages, softcover      Item # 069253*

### Marketing Workbook for Nonprofit Organizations Volume II: Mobilize People for Marketing Success
*by Gary J. Stern*

Put together a successful promotional campaign based on the most persuasive tool of all: personal contact. Learn how to mobilize your entire organization, its staff, volunteers, and supporters in a focused, one-to-one marketing campaign. Comes with *Pocket Guide for Marketing Representatives*. In it, your marketing representatives can record key campaign messages and find motivational reminders.

*192 pages, softcover      Item # 069105*

## Vital Communities

### Community Building: What Makes It Work
*by Wilder Research Center*

Reveals twenty-eight keys to help you build community more effectively. Includes detailed descriptions of each factor, case examples of how they play out, and practical questions to assess your work.

*112 pages, softcover      Item # 069121*

**For current prices, a catalog, or to order call ☎ 800-274-6024**

## Community Economic Development Handbook
*by Mihailo Temali*

A concrete, practical handbook to turning any neighborhood around. It explains how to start a community economic development organization, and then lays out the steps of four proven and powerful strategies for revitalizing inner-city neighborhoods.

*288 pages, softcover*     *Item # 069369*

The Fieldstone Nonprofit Guide to
## Conducting Community Forums
*by Carol Lukas and Linda Hoskins*

Provides step-by-step instruction to plan and carry out exciting, successful community forums that will educate the public, build consensus, focus action, or influence policy.

*128 pages, softcover*     *Item # 069318*

## Funder's Guides

## Community Visions, Community Solutions
Grantmaking for Comprehensive Impact
*by Joseph A. Connor and Stephanie Kadel-Taras*

Helps foundations, community funds, government agencies, and other grantmakers uncover a community's highest aspiration for itself, and support and sustain strategic efforts to get to workable solutions.

*128 pages, softcover*     *Item # 06930X*

## A Funder's Guide to Evaluation: Leveraging
Evaluation to Improve Nonprofit Effectiveness
*Peter York*

This book includes strategies and tools to help grantmakers support and use evaluation as a nonprofit organizational capacity-building tool.

160 pages, softcoverItem # 069482

Strengthening Nonprofit Performance
## A Funder's Guide to Capacity Building
*Paul Connolly and Carol Lukas*

This practical guide synthesizes the most recent capacity building practice and research into a collection of strategies, steps, and examples that you can use to get started on or improve funding to strengthen nonprofit organizations.

*176 pages, softcover*     *Item # 069377*

## Violence Prevention & Intervention

## The Little Book of Peace
*Designed and illustrated by Kelly O. Finnerty*

A pocket-size guide to help people think about violence and talk about it with their families and friends. You may download a free copy of *The Little Book of Peace* from our web site at www.FieldstoneAlliance.org.

*24 pages (minimum order 10 copies)*    *Item # 069083*
*Also available in **Spanish** and **Hmong** language editions.*

## Journey Beyond Abuse: A Step-by-Step Guide to
Facilitating Women's Domestic Abuse Groups
*by Kay-Laurel Fischer, MA, LP,*
*and Michael F. McGrane, LICSW*

Create a program where women increase their understanding of the dynamics of abuse, feel less alone and isolated, and have a greater awareness of channels to safety. This book includes twenty-one group activities that you can combine to create groups of differing length and focus.

*208 pages, softcover*     *Item # 069148*

## Moving Beyond Abuse: Stories and Questions for Women Who Have Lived with Abuse
(Companion guided journal to *Journey Beyond Abuse*)

A series of stories and questions that can be used in coordination with the sessions provided in the facilitator's guide or with the guidance of a counselor in other forms of support.

*88 pages, softcover*     *Item # 069156*

## Foundations for Violence-Free Living:
A Step-by-Step Guide to Facilitating Men's
Domestic Abuse Groups
*by David J. Mathews, MA, LICSW*

A complete guide to facilitating a men's domestic abuse program. Includes twenty-nine activities, detailed guidelines for presenting each activity, and a discussion of psychological issues that may arise out of each activity.

*240 pages, softcover*     *Item # 069059*

**For current prices visit us online at 🖥 www.FieldstoneAlliance.org**

**On the Level**

(Participant's workbook to *Foundations for Violence-Free Living*)

Contains forty-nine worksheets including midterm and final evaluations. Men can record their progress.

*160 pages, softcover      Item # 069067*

**What Works in Preventing Rural Violence**

*by Wilder Research Center*

An in-depth review of eighty-eight effective strategies you can use to prevent and intervene in violent behaviors, improve services for victims, and reduce repeat offenses. This report also includes a Community Report Card with step-by-step directions on how you can collect, record, and use information about violence in your community.

*94 pages, softcover      Item # 069040*

# ORDERING INFORMATION

## Order by phone, fax or online

 **Call** toll-free:  800-274-6024
Internationally:  651-556-4509

 **Fax:** 651-556-4517

 **E-mail:** books@fieldstonealliance.org
**Online**: www.FieldstoneAlliance.org

**Mail:**   Fieldstone Alliance
Publishing Center
60 Plato Boulevard East, Suite 150
St. Paul, MN 55107

## Our NO-RISK guarantee

If you aren't completely satisfied with any book for any reason, simply send it back within 30 days for a full refund.

## Pricing and discounts

For current prices and discounts, please visit our web site at www.FieldstoneAlliance.org or call toll free at 800-274-6024.

## Do you have a book idea?

Fieldstone Alliance seeks manuscripts and proposals for books in the fields of nonprofit management and community development. To get a copy of our author guidelines, please call us at 800-274-6024. You can also download them from our web site at www.FieldstoneAlliance.org

## Visit us online

You'll find information about Fieldstone Alliance and more details on our books, such as table of contents, pricing, discounts, endorsements, and more, at www.FieldstoneAlliance.org.

## Quality assurance

We strive to make sure that all the books we publish are helpful and easy to use. Our major workbooks are tested and critiqued by experts before being published. Their comments help shape the final book and—we trust—make it more useful to you.